D0627115

TWAYNE'S WORLD AUTHORS SERIES
A Survey of the World's Literature

FRANCE

Maxwell Smith
Guerry Professor of French, Emeritus
The University of Chattanooga
Former Visiting Professor in Modern Languages
The Florida State University

EDITOR

Charles Perrault

TWAS 639

Charles Perrault
Engraving after portrait by Lebrun

CHARLES PERRAULT

By Jacques Barchilon
University of Colorado

and

Peter Flinders
Harley School

TWAYNE PUBLISHERS

A DIVISION OF G. K. HALL & CO., BOSTON

Library of Congress Cataloging in Publication Data

Barchilon, Jacques.
Charles Perrault.

(Twayne's world authors series ; TWAS 639. France)
Bibliography: pp. 174–183
Includes index.
1. Perrault, Charles, 1628–1703.   2. Authors,
French—17th century—Biography.   I. Flinders, Peter.
II. Title.   III. Series: Twayne's world authors
series ; TWAS 639.   IV. Series: Twayne's world
authors series. France.
PQ1877.B3   841'.4   [B]   81–4189
ISBN 0–8057–6483–6   AACR2

This one is for Nicole and Paul

Contents

About the Authors

Jacques Barchilon, professor of French at the University of Colorado, was educated in Morocco, France, England, and the United States, obtaining the B.A. from the University of Rochester and the Ph.D. from Harvard University. Before coming to the University of Colorado he taught at Smith College and Brown University. He has also given lectures at some twelve universities on both sides of the Atlantic. During the Second World War, he served in England and France in the Free French Forces. He has obtained grants for his research from the University of Colorado, the American Philosophical Society, and the Fulbright Commission. His publications include a critical edition of the manuscript of Charles Perrault's *Contes*, as well as other editions, a critical volume on the French fairy tale, *Le Conte merveilleux français*, and numerous articles on kindred subjects. His colleagues consider him a scholar of seventeenth-century French literature.

Peter Flinders, teacher of French, graduated from the University of San Francisco and obtained the doctorate from the University of California at Berkeley in 1974. He served in the Peace Corps in Western Africa. He is presently teaching at the Harley School, in Rochester, N. Y. Previously he taught at Canisius College and at the State University of New York at Oswego. His publications include the two volumes of the Perrault *Concordance* (1977–1979), which he coedited in collaboration with Jacques Barchilon and J. Anne Foreman.

Preface

The primary aim of this book is to introduce American readers to a French author of the seventeenth century who is practically unknown, while his fairy tales are known the world over. We have therefore given as comprehensive a portrait of the man and the author as we could. Since the fairy tales are so well known—through countless adaptations and translations—we have devoted two lengthy chapters to them. We have carefully steered away from too much psychoanalytic interpretation, avoiding the tiresome discussion of Freud versus Jung, or vice versa. But we confess that our point of view is more Freudian than Jungian, while we still admit that both systems of analysis can contribute a deeper understanding to the symbolism of fairy tales. This is the first full length critical biography of Perrault in English.

We make no apology if our names occur a few times in the bibliography. Until the past four or five years there never was much critical attention devoted to Perrault in this country. We have, however, listed recent doctoral dissertations on Perrault or the fairy tales that have come to our attention. We make no apology either for including in our bibliography articles and books that analyze Perrault's tales structurally and semiologically. But we have not discussed these articles in the body of our volume. Such criticism tends to become very abstract and obscure in summaries. We believe that a specialized article (which we will try to write) should deal with Perrault as modern critics of the past ten years see him.

In the text of this book the reader will find many quotations from Perrault's prose and poetry. When the text appears in English the translations from the French are our own (unless otherwise indicated). In some cases we have provided both the French text and our English translation. We did it for the enjoyment of our readers who know French. We wanted them to judge for themselves, in those specific passages, whether or not Perrault was as good or as bad as we claimed. Our page references identifying quotes from Perrault—whether in French or in English—correspond to the original French text (unless otherwise indicated).

We have expressed our own opinions, as is our right and responsibility in such a work. Some readers might wish to have more details on some aspects of this portrait of Perrault. The question, for instance, of Perrault's finances. Was Perrault rich or poor? We believe he was probably fairly well-off but that may be irrelevant. What may be very relevant are the facts of his personal life that may shed more light on the circumstances of composition of the fairy tales. We have some facts, but we do not have enough. Professor Marc Soriano has very ingeniously reconstructed Perrault's life and perhaps solved its riddle. The writers of the present book are not sure that the "twin theory" of Charles Perrault and his son can explain everything.

Since this work, like Perrault's tales, is a collaboration, we might help our readers by stating what was written by one, or the other author. Most of chapters 1 through 3 are the result of a close collaboration. The remaining chapters are more the work of the first author.

A complete edition of Perrault's works is sorely needed. It would show the evolution of Perrault's intellectual productions and their basic uniqueness and unity. Whatever the faults of this critical biography, we hope it has accomplished at least two objectives: to reveal a kind of author and person that grows on his readers the more they know him, and to elicit a strong urge to read all his writings, his fairy tales as well as those among his better works we have singled out in this book. Lovers of Boileau will forgive us, we hope, for having somewhat minimized our account of our author's quarrel with his enemy at the Academy. We must add these final words: Perrault very much belongs to France. Yet the rest of the world who has so eagerly adopted him does not generally know how French Perrault was. This is because he is, like many of his seventeenth-century contemporaries, very classical, and therefore universal. But that is not to say that his classicality should shut him—as in a museum—from our midst. On the contrary, as we hope to have shown, he was vital, opinionated, humane, partial, at times rather prejudiced and limited, and at other times extraordinarily perceptive. In a word, he was exciting.

JACQUES BARCHILON
PETER FLINDERS

Acknowledgments

Generous grants are hereby gratefully acknowledged; they came from the University of Colorado Council on Research and Creative Work, the Council for International Exchange of Scholars, and the American Philosophical Society. Thanks also to the Bibliothèque Nationale and to the British Library (especially the Photographic Services). It is with the permission of both these libraries that we have used microfilms provided by them. Ms. Jean Seegraber (Houghton Library, Harvard University) has speedily and gracefully secured many photocopies of Perrault's works for us. The time and effort of many friends and colleagues have been invaluable: Mme. Andrée Kail (French Department, University of Colorado), Michael J. Preston, and Esther Zago (both of the University of Colorado), and finally Mme. J. Anne Foreman (Illinois State University). Peter Flinders (Harley School, Rochester, N. Y.) came to help write this book virtually *in medias res*. The two children of Jacques Barchilon have had much patience with the toils and stresses of their scholar father in travail. The typist, Mrs. Karen Moreira, has struggled beyond the call of ordinary duty with a difficult manuscript and too many revisions.

Chronology

1628 January 12, Charles Perrault born, son of Pierre Perrault, lawyer at the *Parlement* of Paris.

1637 Begins school at the Collège de Beauvais (near the Sorbonne); will always be in the top ranks in all his classes.

1643 Stops attending school at age fifteen; hereafter largely self-taught. First literary attempt: a satirical translation, in burlesque verses, of the sixth book of Vergil's *Aeneid*.

1651 Becomes a lawyer, having fulfilled his requirements; diploma granted from the University of Orléans.

1652 Death of father.

1653 First publication: *Les Murs de Troie ou l'origine du burlesque*, a poem coauthored with his brothers.

1654 Renounces a career in law, becomes a *commis* ("secretary") of his brother Pierre, the tax receiver of Paris; first *vers galants*.

1657 Death of mother.

1659 Two poems: "Portrait d'Iris" and "Portrait de la voix d'Iris."

1660 Beginning of career as occasional or "public poet" devoted to the glories of Louis XIV's reign with the publication of the "Ode sur le Mariage du roi" and "Ode sur la paix"; publication of the allegorical work, *Dialogue de l'Amour et de l'Amitié*.

1661 Poem on the birth of the first royal offspring: "Ode au roi sur la naissance de Mgr le Dauphin"; *Le Miroir ou la Métamorphose d'Oronte*.

1663 Appointed secretary to Colbert's "little council," or "petite académie," later the Académie des Inscriptions et Belles-Lettres. "Discours sur l'acquisition de Dunkerque par le roi."

1668 On the royal payroll for the first time as *Premier Commis des Bâtiments*. *La Peinture* and *Le Parnasse poussé à bout*.

1671 Becomes member of the French Academy.

1672 Elected *Chancelier* of the Academy. Granted the *charge* ("commission") of *Contrôleur des Bâtiments de Sa Majesté*.

1672 Marries Marie Guichon, age nineteen.

1675 Baptism of Charles-Samuel, Perrault's first son. *Recueil de divers ouvrages en prose et en vers*.

1676 Baptism of second son, Charles.

1678 Baptism of third son, Pierre, to whom the famous tales will be attributed in 1695 and 1697. Death of wife at age twenty-five.

1681 Elected *Directeur* of the French Academy.

1683 Death of Colbert. Dismissed from government service.

1686 *Saint Paulin évêque de Nole, avec une épitre chrétienne sur la pénitence et une ode aux nouveaux convertis*, a poem consisting of six *chants*, dedicated to Bossuet.

1687 The Quarrel of the Ancients and Moderns begins with Charles's reading of a poem, *Le Siècle de Louis le Grand*.

1688 "Le Génie, épitre à M. de Fontenelle"; *Parallèle des Anciens et des Modernes en ce qui regarde les arts et les sciences, dialogues*; "A Mgr le Dauphin sur la prise de Philippsbourg, ode."

1690 *Le Cabinet des Beaux-Arts, ou Recueil d'estampes gravées d'après les tableaux d'un plafond où les Beaux-Arts sont représentés*, a series of prose commentaries on paintings which decorated Perrault's own residence; *Parallèle des Anciens et des Modernes en ce qui regarde l'éloquence*.

1691 *La Marquise de Salusses ou la Patience de Griselidis*, published subsequently as part of the *Contes*.

1692 *Parallèle des Anciens et des Modernes en ce qui regarde la Poésie*, and two poems: *La Chasse* and *La Création du Monde*.

1693 *Les Souhaits ridicules* (in the periodical *Le Mercure Galant*).

1694 *Apologie des femmes*, a poem in defense of women; *Peau d'Ane*, the first fairy tale (in verse) of Perrault.

1695 Dedication manuscript of "Contes de Ma Mère l'Oye" [Tales of Mother Goose].

1696 *Les Hommes illustres qui ont paru en France pendant ce*

CHAPTER 1

Life

I Early Years

IT is difficult in this century to visualize the France and the Paris of Charles Perrault's birth. Let us try, nevertheless, to reconstruct the historical atmosphere of his early years, if only because they were those of a man whose *Contes de Ma Mère l'Oye* [Tales of Mother Goose] were to influence generation after generation of children throughout the world. The day of his birth, January 12, 1628, is not significant in itself, but the year is, for it was in 1628 that an historic event occurred which symbolized the growing power of the monarchy. That was the capture and dismantling of the Huguenot Atlantic stronghold of La Rochelle. The seaport had rebelled and had sought help from Protestant England, a political sin that neither the king, Louis XIII, nor his powerful prime minister, Cardinal Richelieu, could forgive. This was certainly not an age of religious toleration. There was no modern separation of church and state, and Roman Catholicism was the only official religion when Richelieu crushed the Huguenots by destroying their Atlantic stronghold. The French monarchy had begun a long process of religious repression which would culminate, during Perrault's lifetime, in the final expulsion of the Protestants with the Revocation of the Edict of Nantes (1685).[1] The siege of La Rochelle was important for his parents, although the child Perrault came into the world unconscious of an event that was later to have great bearing upon him and his fellow Frenchmen.

As we sketch these formative years of Perrault, we should dwell a moment on the unusual circumstances of his biological arrival. Charles had a twin brother, François, who came into the world a few minutes before him, and who died when only six

19

months of age. A French professor and critic, Marc Soriano, places great importance upon what he considers the writer's obsession with his deceased twin brother. We will return to the "twin situation" in later pages of this book. For the time being, it is sufficient to say that at six months of age the infant Charles may have been seriously impressed, or even traumatized, by the death of his brother. In his analyses Marc Soriano seems to find echoes of the lost twin in practically every page Perrault wrote.[2]

We have some details concerning Perrault's childhood, as he recounts it in his *Mémoires de ma vie* [Memories of My Life], which was written a few years before his death for his children, and not intended for publication. His mother taught him to read. He seems to have been warmly nurtured in a fairly well-to-do bourgeois family. His father Pierre was a lawyer-magistrate at the Paris Parlement, an important legislative institution of the old monarchy. There were other children in the family, a sister, Marie, who died at thirteen, and four older brothers—Jean, the eldest, also a lawyer but little known (he died in 1669); Pierre (1611–1680), the tax collector, who will help Charles in later life; Claude (1613–1688), well-known in his time as a doctor-architect; and Nicolas (1624–1662), the priest, a doctor of theology and professor at the Sorbonne, but eventually excluded from that body for his Jansenist views.

Our author was a member of a large, well-established family, fairly close-knit as most French families still are today. He entered school at the age of eight, which seems none too young by today's standards. His father helped him with his studies by making him recite his lessons at night. Perrault tells us that during his school years he was never whipped by his teachers at the Collège de Beauvais in Paris which he attended, as had all his brothers before him. In his *Mémoires* he tells us also about the importance of Latin in his education. It was, after all, the main language used throughout the schools of Europe for centuries. Absurd as it may sound to a modern ear, Perrault may be said to have learned French by learning Latin. In any case, he was always among the top students in most of his classes. It is ironic that he professed to write poetry rather than prose as a student, because it would be through his prose, not his poetry, that his name would be remembered three centuries after his death.

II *Dropping Out*

Charles Perrault was not the most assiduous or respectful of students in his last year at school, the year devoted to philosophy. At that time he must have been fifteen years old. He often quarreled with his teacher, reproaching him for not giving him enough occasion to talk or to debate in class. One day during class, Perrault formally took leave of his teacher, in the middle of an argument, never to return. A friend named Beaurain joined him in his protest and walked out with him. Thereafter, Perrault was completely self-taught. For three or four years he studied with Beaurain. Their choice of reading was unusually serious for adolescents free to read as they pleased. They chose the Bible (in French, presumably) and the *Histoire de France* by La Serre, plus a series of Latin authors, Tertullianus, Vergil, and Cornelius Nepos. "And most of the other classical authors," Perrault adds, referring to the familiar Latin curriculum of his century.

We have no record of his parents' thinking that their son's freedom was wrong nor that his attitude towards authority in "dropping out" was reprehensible. The way in which he obtained his *Licence,* or law diploma, at Orléans, suggests that at that time "degrees were granted with scandalous readiness."[3] It happened at night, at the University of Orléans. Apparently Charles and his fellow students woke up the examiners who arrived in the hall with their academic gowns and caps over their night clothes. If the candlelight scene seems to us highly bizarre, it also seemed so to Perrault himself who recalls the examining committee of three professors as the judges of Hell: "It was like Minos, Aecus, and Rhadamantes coming to interrogate ghosts."[4] The examination was a perfunctory oral battle of wits about Roman law, in Latin, between examiners and students. That one could *buy* the diplomas by paying the professors after the examination perhaps explains the perfunctoriness of the ceremony. When Perrault obtained his law degree in 1651, he was twenty-three years old.

His first literary efforts were made during the same period. These were verses in the burlesque genre, a rewriting of classical works in a familiar and jocular manner (for instance, Jupiter asking his wife Juno for his slippers). This genre was all the rage,

practiced by many authors. Only one of these, however, Paul
Scarron, survives as a burlesque author. His *Énéide travestie*
(1648) still finds appreciative readers today. The burlesque style
is generally "culture-bound" and depends for its comic effects
upon a certain familiarity with the work parodied. The first attempt of Perrault, his friend Beaurain, and his two brothers, was
a burlesque rendition of the sixth book of Vergil's *Aeneid*, that
famous Latin epic poem about the foundation of Rome, "a thing
rather too sacred for parody," according to Andrew Lang.[5] At
that time they were still full of youthful rebellion and found a
ready outlet in such satirical endeavors.

In our judgment this early effort falls flat. The work is much
too full of topical allusions, and it offers a quantity of scatological
puns that smack of the kind of jokes liked by French medical
students and adolescents. It was not published in Perrault's lifetime, but in 1901, through the efforts of Paul Bonnefon, who secured a manuscript of the text. Not much more needs be said
concerning this inferior work of youthful petulance. The scatological element itself (the four-letter words, the references to bodily
functions providing unusual rhyming effects) we must ascribe
to a kind of childish regression by the three brothers: Nicolas,
the future priest and doctor in theology, then in his late twenties;
Claude, already a physician in his mid-thirties; and Charles himself. In such a collective work, one should not attempt to at-
tribute too many of the best, or of the worst, lines to Charles
himself, and we must remember that the *Mémoires* clearly state
that Claude was the author of more lines of poetry than either
one of the other two brothers. It was mostly his work, not
Charles's. The value of this episode is in what it reveals about
this long-gone happy family of brothers collaborating in a joy-
ously free Rabelaisian vein.

This brotherly cooperation continued for yet another and last
joint satirical venture, the *Murs de Troye, ou l'origine du Burlesque* [The Walls of Troy, or the origin of the Burlesque], which
was published in 1653. This mediocre work about how Troy was
built is an overlong series of flat octosyllabic lines. It has lin-
guistic and documentary merits in that it belongs to the history
of the genre.[6] The work enables us to see the continuity of Perrault's satirical bent in later works. In *Peau d'Ane* [Donkey-skin],

"La Belle au bois dormant" [Sleeping Beauty] or "Cendrillon" [Cinderella], we find the same unerring instinct for the catchy word "à la mode," the same sense of the picturesque so peculiar to Perrault.

III *Closer to the Sun*

The early life of Charles Perrault was not extraordinary: he had a fairly happy childhood and adolescence, although his education seems somewhat unorthodox, first obtaining his law degree and then dabbling in a rather ephemeral satirical genre. As the last born among brothers, all fairly well-gifted and provided for, he fitted well in the family. Fate was to give him a fortuitous nudge at the right moment.

He did not practice law very much and took only two or three cases. He did not really need to work but was employed by his own elder brother Pierre in 1654. He was then twenty-six years old. Pierre Perrault had just purchased the office of *Receveur Général des Finances de Paris* (tax collector for the City of Paris). Charles did not have much to do except run errands for his brother, collecting money from taxpayers and depositing sums in various branches of the royal treasury. His leisure time was spent reading voraciously in the large library of his brother.

Charles was happy in the service of his brother until 1664. At that time he circulated his first *précieux* poems, "Portrait d'Iris," "Portrait de la voix d'Iris" [Portrait of Iris, Portrait of Iris's voice]. *Préciosité* is both a literary mode and a literary moment. Perrault was an avid practitioner of *préciosité* during its greatest vogue (1655–1670). These poems gave him a certain reputation among various minor poets as a published author, a writer of delicate and fashionable little elegies and odes in the taste of the period: polished, reserved, mildly erotic *galanteries*. He versified, almost too easily, line upon line of this kind of poetry. It does not read well today, sounding flat to the ear, in contrast with his prose which rings true with the sound of an authentic voice. A charming prose work, *Le Dialogue de l'Amour et de l'Amitié* [The Dialog between Love and Friendship, 1660], whose title is self-explanatory, foreshadows the fairy tales of later years. This allegorical work is dedicated to the great critic of the theater, the

Abbé d'Aubignac, and contains a lively letter of dedication which is in itself another tale of four pages concerning the union of goodness and beauty. The resultant offspring of this wedding is friendship (*l'amitié*).

During the period that Perrault was producing these innocuous love poems, he had already begun his career of public poet, extolling the person, the glories, and the reign of the Sun King. Various poems celebrate either the recently concluded peace with Spain, "Ode sur la paix" [Ode on Peace], the wedding of the king with the Spanish Infanta, Marie-Thérèse, "Ode sur le mariage du roi," [Ode on the Wedding of the King], or the birth of the first royal child, "Ode au roi sur la naissance de Mgr le Dauphin" [Ode to the King on the Birth of My Lord the Dauphin]. These works appeared during the years 1660–1661, which marked the beginning of Louis XIV's reign and in England the Restoration of the Stuarts in Charles II. The life of Charles Perrault will now become intimately involved with a monarchy at once enlightened (in its patronage of outstanding artists, writers, and scientists) and chauvinistic (in its exaggerated worship of the French king as the embodiment of the French nation). Nevertheless, in the world of three centuries ago, which for Europeans was Europe alone, France was a most powerful nation. Louis XIV commanded the most populous nation in Europe and was determined to make his mark on the world.

Charles Perrault was happy to live in this era and eventually became its panegyrist. He listened, he read, he observed, and he remembered his contemporaries and their deeds long after their passing. While he had already composed public poetry, he had no official function in the government. However, in 1663, Colbert, the all powerful minister of finances and superintendent of royal buildings, appointed him his secretary. Perrault soon became his factotum, trusted advisor, and *homme de confiance*. At that time he had just turned thirty-five. A fine portrait of Perrault by Le Brun in 1665 reveals a dashingly handsome young man: fine features, straight nose, thick eyebrows, penetrating dark eyes, a slight quizzical smile about the mouth, the whole face framed by luxurious locks of black hair cascading down the shoulders. Let us not forget the thin moustache, as if to suggest that this man wanted to sport the same appearance as his master and king Louis XIV.

What were Perrault's duties? It seems that Colbert did not trust his own judgment in artistic and literary matters and, as a result, relied mainly on Perrault's advice. One of the most pressing issues at hand was the royal residence of the Louvre, which was due for massive renovation. Perrault unwittingly found himself at one of those crossroads of art history. His influence and taste oriented the artistic life and tastes of France away from the Italian baroque style and decidedly toward classicism or neo-classicism. In a period when all Europe looked to Italian masters for artistic leadership, it was natural for Colbert to invite the last great artist and architect of the Renaissance, Lorenzo Bernini, to provide a grand design for the royal palace. In Colbert's mind floated a vast vision of obelisks, pyramids, triumphal arches, and mausoleums. In the minds of those Frenchmen who may have known Rome there was perhaps the idea of imitating the style of the Eternal City. The issue is complex and debated. Bernini did come to Paris and was treated with great deference. His designs and plans for a monumental facade for the Louvre were adopted, the foundations were built, and the illustrious architect, provided with munificent monetary rewards, left for Rome.

Thereafter everything went awry. Construction stopped. A new design, apparently the result of the collaboration between three architects—Le Vau, D'Orbay, and Claude Perrault, the brother of Charles—was adopted. It is that of the Louvre we see today. We note especially the eastern facade, known, rightly or wrongly, as the Perrault colonnade. In his *Mémoires*, Charles writes that the idea for the imposing row of coupled Corinthian columns was his, and the complex engineering, the blueprints, were those of his brother Claude. Throughout Paris and beyond, the influence of this design was enormous. From that time up to our own, buildings and churches with similar Greek colonnades kept appearing. The style spread through Europe, even crossing the Atlantic, and many American banks and museums of the nineteenth and early twentieth centuries can be traced to that early model of the Louvre.

For the next twenty years Perrault was one of the busiest men of the French kingdom. He was in some ways fulfilling the functions of a twentieth-century minister of cultural affairs, but he busied himself with far more minutiae than a minister. He advised the poets who wrote poems celebrating official events. There is record of a rather piquant encounter between Charles Perrault and a young budding poet, who would one day become very famous, Jean Racine. On the occasion of the wedding of Louis XIV with the Spanish Princess Marie-Thérèse, Perrault had published a poem celebrating the occasion. Racine also composed a poem at the same time and had sought the advice both of the poet-critic Jean Chapelain and of Perrault. This is not the time to discuss the relative merits of Racine's poem. Rather, we simply will quote Racine's own words: "he [Perrault] objects . . . to my comparison of Venus and Mars . . . because Venus is a prostitute. . . ." Racine had compared Louis XIV to Mars and the Spanish princess to Venus. Even though he changed the passage, Racine did not appreciate Perrault's lack of poetic perception, for "when poets speak of the Gods, they refer to them as divine beings, and consequently like perfect beings. . . ."[7]

Quite clearly, Perrault had erred in the literality of his judgment. He and Racine diverged diametrically in their temperament and tastes. While Racine became the great author of classical tragedies we read today, Perrault continued in his career as public servant for nearly two decades, yet he was always contributing to the literature of his time. In 1671 he became a member of the French Academy. Since Colbert had urged him to be a candidate and since he was elected in spite of a somewhat small output of work, Perrault felt pressured during the next few years to continue writing. But most of his activities were devoted to "buildings and grounds." Among his responsibilities were keeping the books and paying the architects and workmen who were building the Louvre and Versailles. To this day, notes written and signed by him, instructing the Treasury to pay designated sums, still turn up at rare book and manuscript sales. He was also concerned with painters and sculptors, since he was a member of, or counselor to, the "petite" Academy of Painting and Sculpture, the forerunner of the still existing Académie des Inscriptions et Belles Lettres.

The Bibliothèque Nationale in Paris has an impressive quantity of manuscript material from our author's pen, as well as correspondence addressed to him. One letter of Perrault to Colbert is a recommendation for a nobleman, Monsieur de Severac, who wanted a position as officer in the king's navy (March 17, 1673); another letter to Colbert is a lengthy technical comparison of French and English ships (August 26, 1675); and in another letter addressed to Perrault, the Italian actor Cinthio requested funds to defray a journey to Rome, Venice, Ferrara, and Bologna in order to recruit Italian actors for the royal stage. In letters sent to the sculptor Girardon studying in Rome, Perrault requested the shipment of "slaves extraordinarily handsome of body who could be used as models for our academy here" (July 19, 1667).

During the same year that he became officially the *Contrôleur des Bâtiments de Sa Majesté*, he married, at age forty-four, the nineteen-year-old Marie Guichon. We have a lively account of his wedding through the letters sent home to Holland by the scientist Christian Huygens.[8] The bride was a beautiful brunette, the entertainment was lavish, the crowd numerous, and the pair of lovers happy to have found each other. If it was not love at first sight, we can be sure it came later. There were at least three children, all boys, born in 1675, 1676, and 1678. The name of the third son, Pierre, is the one whose name will later be associated with the famous fairy tales. It seems there may have been a fourth child, "Mademoiselle Perrault," mentioned in 1695 by a relative of Perrault, Mlle. L'Héritier.[9]

While he was married, Perrault lived in a rather sumptuous residence in a section of Paris which is still fashionable, and still well-preserved, the Palais-Royal. His marital happiness was suddenly shattered by the death of his wife in October, 1678. She apparently died of smallpox. He regretted this loss deeply all his life and it must have been the beginning of a painful transition in his existence. He was fifty years old, a widower, with at least three young children to educate in a motherless home.

As we look into French history we find that in 1678 a war with Holland had just ended. Racine, after the production of

Phèdre, had abandoned the stage to become with Boileau the royal historiographer. Persecution of the French Jansenists had begun anew; and a scandalous trial was going on, which proved the connection of Mme de Montespan, the royal mistress, with a Paris gang of poisoners and diabolists. Altogether it does not impress us as a particularly brilliant period of the age of Louis XIV.

We can safely assume that Perrault devoted more time to his children since he was at home more than before. He had also achieved some kind of literary reputation. His *Recueil de divers ouvrages* [Collection of Various Works] was beautifully copied in a sumptuously illustrated manuscript and published, in 1675 and 1676.

IV *The Creative Last Years*

Perrault worked for Colbert for just four years following the death of his wife. The influence of Colbert on Louis XIV could not prevent the king from moving the court to Versailles. The construction of the Louvre was abandoned, and colossal sums, which Colbert did not approve of, were lavished on the suburban palace. In the same year (1682) that the king moved, Perrault made ready to relinquish his post. The following year Colbert died and Perrault's name was erased from the list of writers and artists who were receiving yearly stipends from the government. While he was a member of the French Academy for life, he was removed from the other *petite académie* of arts and architecture.

The last twenty years of Perrault's life were truly his golden years. This reasonably pacific man soon became embroiled in a major literary dispute, which we will discuss subsequently in detail, the *Querelle des Anciens et des Modernes* [Quarrel of the Ancients and the Moderns]. Briefly stated, it was a polemic in which there were two sides: the Moderns were those critics and writers who would readily admit that their century, the seventeenth, was a century whose productions in the arts and sciences were equal if not superior to those of Greek and Latin antiquity; the Ancients held the opposite point of view. From the perspective of three hundred years, this quarrel may seem pompously academic. In reality, it was the beginning of a new, "modern" aesthetic sense.

These years brought out the best and also some of Perrault's worst literary works. Among the best, we must mention the *Parallèle des Anciens et des Modernes* [Parallel of the Ancients and the Moderns, 1688–1697]; *Les Hommes illustres* [Illustrious Men of this Century, published in 1696–1700]; *Apologie des femmes* [The Vindication of Wives, published in 1694]; *Mémoires de ma vie* (not intended for publication but published posthumously in 1759 and again in 1909); and of course, his most famous work, the immortal fairy tales, which brought him world fame, *Histoires ou Contes du temps passé* (1697). This does not exclude the three verse tales, *Griselidis* [Griselda], *Peau d'Ane* [Donkey-Skin] and *Les Souhaits ridicules* [The Ridiculous Wishes]. His not so outstanding works were his religious poems, such as *Saint Paulin* and *Adam ou la Création de l'homme* [Adam, or the Creation of Man].

A somewhat tragic affair obscures the year in which the fairy tales were published, 1697. His last born son, Pierre, the gifted boy to whom the stories are attributed in collaboration with his father, became involved in a quarrel and subsequently killed a young neighbor with his sword. At that time Pierre was nineteen years old. Documents available today tell of a trial, indemnities, and other reparations the father had proposed to pay the mother of the deceased boy. Was it really a quarrel? Who provoked whom? The data at hand are not conclusive and some elements of this judicial puzzle are apparently missing from the records.[10]

The "child prodigy who became a delinquent," as Marc Soriano describes him, did not live long. A lieutenant in the Régiment Dauphin, one of the elite corps of the royal army, he died in 1700, presumably during some engagement. Pierre was only twenty-two years old at the time of his death, outlived by his father, who died three years later.

Charles Perrault himself had already started to write his *Mémoires*, which he did not finish, and which do not go beyond the early years of his retirement, from 1683 to 1685. He was also writing a collection of reflections entitled "Pensées chrétiennes" [Christian Thoughts], which was partly published early in this century.[11] He was active until the end of his life and faithfully attended the meetings of the French Academy. By the standards of his time, his life was exceptionally long. Perrault lived past his seventy-fifth birthday and died peacefully during the night of May 15, 1703. At his funeral, Charles, his second son, and Samuel René Guichon, priest and brother of Perrault's deceased wife, were present.[12]

We know that there was quite a vogue for fairy tales in the last five years of the seventeenth century. Perrault had imitators in his century, during the next, and perhaps even today. However, there will always be a certain mystery attached to Perrault's fame. While he was alive, he had been ridiculed by Boileau for having written meaningless and childish stories, unworthy of the attention of a serious writer. Yet these "meaningless" stories are among the most meaningful ever written and link Perrault's name to the mythology, folklore, and psychology of modern man. That he may have died without realizing he had written a world classic suggests perhaps a little ironic tragedy, typical, in a way, of a Racinian play. That his work lives on is fortunate for us, the readers, in that we may continue to study the man. The *oeuvres* reveal the conscience and soul of the writer. And to his works we now turn.

CHAPTER 2

The Précieux *Poet and the Public Servant*

I   *The Early Burlesque Phase*

PERRAULT, from an early age, showed a definite tendency to follow the fashions and the trends of his day. He began with satirical versions of classical works. Inspired by this mode were the *Énéide burlesque* and the *Murs de Troye ou l'origine du burlesque,* which shall not long detain us here, because their tone and form do not seem to have survived the test of centuries. In the main, they are unreadable today.

Granted that the satirical style of these burlesque poems is dated, they still exhibit a very rich command of the resources of the French language. For instance, the *Murs de Troye* contains a large number of words pertaining to masonry and architecture, slang expressions, various references to the costumes of the period, the language of the law, and numerous arts and crafts. This burlesque phase shows a talent for verbal exuberance, the inverse form of the *précieux* style. The literary technique of the burlesque is an attempt to create comical effects by reducing to the trivial, popular, or vulgar level, themes and characters of a higher, more refined, even royal order. Both modes of stylistic approach seem to us to correspond to the baroque period. Sometimes we do not know from which part of his personality Perrault is writing, the irreverent and burlesque, or the refined and more lyrical side. Forty-five years after this youthful parodic phase, Perrault, in the fairy tales, wrote of magical transformations of lizards into liveried lackeys straight and erect on Cinderella's coach. This ambiguous use of language describing animals in human terms, or humans in animal garb, has a long tradition in the creation of comical burlesque effects,

31

from Aesop's *Fables* to Walt Disney's Mickey Mouse, by way
of La Fontaine's "Ant and the Grasshopper," Edward Lear's
"The Owl and the Pussycat," and more recently, James Thurber's
special rendition of "Little Red Riding Hood."[1]

II *Perrault and* Préciosité

Préciosité is one of those terms that seem to need redefinition
with each successive generation of poets. We can accept the
general idea that this mode of literary expression is the refinement of thought resulting from a learned use of words, the appli-
cation of intelligence to knowledge, and the cultivation of psychological insight into feelings, a renewing of language through
metaphor, a certain fascination with the exquisitely difficult
turn of phrase, the sublimation of erotic drives through ingenious language. Essentially, it is concerned with expression
of love through abstraction, symbols, and oblique references.[2]

None of the anthologies of *précieux* poetry mention Perrault,
or even quote any of his verses. Of his first published poems, "Le
Portrait d'Iris" and the "Portrait de la voix d'Iris" (1659), Paul
Bonnefon writes that these works are written "in facile verses,
without personal accents, which were very well-liked by contemporary readers because they suited well the taste of the
moment."[3] The next work written in the *précieux* mode that
was published in 1660 is in prose: *Dialogue de l'Amour et de
l'Amitié*. It was very well received, often reprinted, translated
into Italian, and even transcribed in a beautiful velum manuscript for the library of the finance minister Fouquet.

At that time, Perrault had been introduced to Fouquet, the
then great patron of French art. At Vaux-le-Vicomte, Fouquet's
sumptuous château and model for Versailles, he met La Fontaine,
Molière, and other now well-known cultural luminaries. He
found himself among some of the poets whose names would
become famous in the following centuries. At that time he was
their equal, a beginner himself. The light tone, the liveliness
of the repartees in the *Dialogue*—all these aspects provide a
foretaste of the later Perrault of the *Contes*. One passage in
particular is especially noteworthy, one in which he describes
love's blindness. The character Love speaks and explains that

she puts in front of the lovers' eyes certain magical crystals
or lenses: "These crystals have the power to correct the defects
of objects and to reduce them to their just proportions. If a
woman's eyes are too small, or a forehead too small, I put in
front of her lover's eye a crystal which enlarges things, so that
he sees her eyes as pleasantly enlarged and her forehead reasonably broad."[4] In the tale of "Riquet à la houppe" [Rickey with
the Tuft], published in 1697, we will find the same idea and
practically the same words when Perrault wittily explains that
there was no magic transformation of the ugly Riquet at the
end of the story. This, and the passage quoted above, are
simply illustrations of the typically *précieux* idea that "beauty
is in the eye of the beholder." The princess, being in love with
him, no longer saw his deformities and was thus ready to marry
him.

Perrault can consistently rhyme or write about love with a
certain felicity, even if today we find little to admire; here
is a typical example:

> In shame discreet and wise
> A blush rose to her face
> Which, with raised hand, she thought to hide;
> But a little sigh, true witness to her flame,
> From her breast taking flight,
> The secret of her soul did bare.[5]

This is an apt and ingenious poetic rendition of the silent
language of love. Flame is here both a sensual reference to the
heat of blushing as well as a reference to the reddening of the
face. A silent sigh speaks louder than words, letting out the
secret of the young lady's heart and soul.

While this passage lends itself easily to interpretation, it is
a clear statement of the irrepressibility of the emotions; other
passages are more strictly ambiguous, a characteristic of the
précieux and poetic mode. Here, in a discussion between Venus
and her son Eros, we invite the reader to evaluate for himself the
true meaning of the goddess's admonition to her son:

One day while Venus was discussing with her son important affairs
of state and seeing him disposed to listen to remonstrances she had

been contemplating for a long time, she spoke to him thus: "You are my son, the most powerful among the Gods, all obey your laws, and there are no mortals so barbaric as to not recognize you as their sovereign. But so long as your subjects are as miserable as they are, you cannot derive much glory from the vast extent of your kingdom. Believe me, the grandeur of a monarch is not always measured by the breadth of his lands, and one looks much less to the number of obedient subjects than to the felicity he has procured for them. However, one sees only unhappy people in your land; only a people incessantly complaining, groaning, sighing, and wishing death upon themselves at every moment in order to be delivered of their sufferings."[6]

Granted that this passage has been lifted out of context, it can nevertheless be interpreted either as a reflection of the political state of any kingdom or, at face value, as a manifest recommendation for more kindness in the distribution and uses of love among lovers. Therefore, when Venus says to her son, "You are the most powerful among the Gods, all obey your laws . . . ," Perrault might have been thinking of the mythological figure of Glory speaking to her most illustrious son, Louis XIV, urging him toward more justice among his subjects. Furthermore, Perrault indicates indirect praise of the king, inferring that a king is great because he attends to the welfare of his subjects, not because he rules over millions of them. However, in context, it is a reprimand with the implication that this ideal, in fact, is not always the case. Such possibilities of interpretations on two, or more, levels are the essence of poetic ambiguity, characteristic of other poets of his century, small and great alike, such as Voiture, Racan, Saint-Amant, Sarasin, Corneille, Racine, and La Fontaine.

In the works of such a prolific poet as Perrault, so attuned to the moods and fashions of his day, it would have been surprising if we did not find echoes of La Fontaine and Racine. In some of Perrault's lesser known, indeed, generally unknown works, one finds surprisingly beautiful verse. These lines treating of a theme dear to the *précieux* literature of the time, that of unrequited love, reach a tonality equal to that of Racine:

> I knew to what extent you were inhuman,
> And I saw that your heart flaming with anger

Was no less cruel than your eyes were tender. . . .
And since I had the misfortune to displease you,
I have known but moans, hopeless tears,
And everlasting pains. . . .
This black son of Chagrin and Impatience,
Displaying the pain of my long suffering,
And the unspeakable excess of your cruelty
Made clear, without shame, to my wretched heart,
Your more fortunate suitors midst love's pleasures.[7]

We are not saying that Perrault is consistently equal to Racine or La Fontaine, but, at times, in the realm of lyrical and *précieux* verse, he can measure up to them.

III   *The Public Poet and Civil Servant*

It was by way of his "official" prose and poetry that Perrault came to be noticed first by the critic Jean Chapelain who was advisor to Colbert and who introduced him to the powerful minister. The celebration of events in the life of kings and queens seems strange to us now, but three centuries ago, in Perrault's France, the person of the king embodied for the populace as well as for the more "elevated" classes any patriotic feelings they may have nourished. The official poems of Perrault are dedicated to such momentous events in the life of Louis XIV as marriages, births, war (or peace), sicknesses, recoveries, and so on. Let us name a few: "Ode sur la paix; Ode sur le mariage du roi" (1660); and "Ode au roi sur la naissance de Mgr le Dauphin" (1661). To these three poems we should add an official prose work, celebrating the purchase of Dunkirk from England, "Discours sur l'acquisition de Dunquerque" [On the Purchase of Dunkirk, 1663].

Perrault wrote fifteen such works, very few of which are readable today. Their interest is only historical or topical. If we single out those which still have some literary merit, we should say a few words about the "Ode sur le mariage du roi" (1660). In short lines well suited to the joyful occasion, Perrault describes Louis XIV as a child: "It was he who even in childhood / Was obeyed in all places / Less by the right of his (divine) birth / Than by the power of his eyes."[8] While this is not Racine, or La Fontaine, the rhyme reads easily and seems authentic. It is, after all, nothing other than poetry of official praise. Here are the last lines of the poem: "How sweet the allurements of that charming bride / When lit by the torch of Love. / Extinguish, proud Sun, your untimely light / And make way for Night more beautiful than Day."[9] Rather harmonious and mildly erotic, these lines could be found worthy of La Fontaine's *Adonis* or of his *Psyché* and, quoted out of context, might even confuse a critic. In the midst of a "patriotic" piece there can be found passages with an authentic voice and feeling.

IV *War and Peace*

In January, 1668, Louis XIV conducted a short and apparently successful campaign to recover a Spanish province, then part of the Netherlands. At that time winter campaigns were thought impossible. Nevertheless, he conquered what was then called Franche-Comté, pushing the French frontier all the way to the Jura Mountains. This was the occasion of a short book by Perrault, *Le Parnasse poussé à bout* [Parnassus cornered, 1668], this time a mélange of prose and poetry. It is a felicitously written counterpoint of contrasting tones. The prose passages tell of an expedition in search of the king by Calliope (the muse of history) together with the poet. They are looking for the French army which is advancing too fast. There are spirited dialogues with such symbolic figures as Fame, Terror, Bellone (the goddess of war). There are moments of sheer joy when the soldiers recognize their young king among them. The whole poem has an atmosphere of heady enthusiasm, the realism of some descriptions balanced by passages of allegorical fantasy, such as Victory gliding over the battlefield. The prose passages have a characteristic alertness. This kind of poem anticipates the later fairy tales, in that the use of allegorical figures was already a sort of reference to a supernatural poetic world in which a thinly veiled fiction of a dreamlike world created mythological counterparts of reality. Perrault, and other poets of his age, constantly developed the symbolic convention that their king was a personification of Jupiter, with all his godlike powers and prerogatives. All the arts of the period—painting, sculpture, and music—

referred to the king and his entourage as living, so to speak, a mythological dream.

One cannot stress enough the extent of this mythological stylization of the monarchy: a return to antiquity, or rather, a resurrection of it. The expression, "Paris, France, la Rome moderne," became a cliché for seventeenth-century French artists.

That same year (1668), an ingenious, lengthy, and somewhat original poem. *La Peinture* [Painting], praises the art of painting by praising those painters who glorified the reign of Louis XIV. This is ostensibly the main theme of the poem. With our privilege of hindsight, we find Perrault's argumentation the weakest part of the poem, especially his praise of Le Brun, whose art seems flat and academic compared to that of his contemporaries Poussin, La Tour, or Le Lorrain. Le Brun, whose frescoes and paintings cover so many walls and ceilings of Versailles, was a second-rate painter but a first class decorator. His efforts to coordinate interior design are everywhere in the palace of the king. Perrault erred in praising him. The ingeniousness and originality of the poem lie elsewhere.

When he forgot his intent to praise Le Brun, Perrault seized upon some interesting and well-expressed mythological fictions. He compares God to the First Painter, the Arch Creator of all landscapes and colors: "The Sovereign Master of Heaven and Earth paints / With a bold stroke in the void of space / With a blinding flash."[10]

At the end of the poem, Perrault imagined a fiction on the origin of painting. A lover, despairing at the thought of not seeing her soon-to-leave companion, instinctively copied his profile as she saw it silhouetted against the wall of a cave lit by the rays of sunset. All in all, the poem is overlong. We understand, however, how it must have pleased many contemporaries with its "official line" of praise for contemporary art. Perrault proclaimed with conviction that the arts of his century, and especially painting, had never before produced so many masterpieces. This was Perrault's opinion of the supremacy of modern art, to which he would return consistently throughout his life.

Perrault was conscious of belonging to his period as if it

were one of the greatest in French history. Because he had that conviction and could write fairly easily in prose or poetry, he was naturally the editor regularly chosen by his "boss" Colbert for much "propaganda" writing. In this capacity, for example, he was the editor in charge of collecting a volume of poems in honor of the deceased Cardinal Mazarin (*Éloges du Cardinal Mazarin,* 1666). Of course, Perrault's sonnet in praise of Mazarin is to be found on the first page.

He had also edited one of the most luxuriously illustrated books of the century, the account of the festivities the king gave in honor of Mlle de la Vallière in 1662. The volume was entitled *Courses de têtes faites par le roi et par les princes et seigneurs,* published in 1670 [Carousel of 1662]. Since the main event of the festivities was a carousel, there were many costumes, many parades, many dances and ballets. The alert prose of Perrault, versatile and suited for every occasion, narrates all that took place. It is a precious document, a glimpse of the social life and glitter of a joyous and ceremonial moment in the life of seventeenth-century France, which Perrault felicitously recorded. By then, in 1670, Perrault had been a trusted advisor and confident of Colbert for more than seven years; officially he was *Premier Commis,* or private secretary. It was a delicate position. He had the ear of the most powerful minister in France, and his fellow writers knew it.

V *Perrault and the French Academy*

Perrault was one of the busiest men in France and yet found time to write. While he was generally well liked, and was one of the early friends of Racine, there was one man who did not like his writings at all, the critic Boileau. To him, Perrault was a *précieux,* a practitioner of an older style, which he hated. There was a great divergence of temperament between the two. Nevertheless, in spite of any antipathy Boileau may have had for him, Perrault was duly elected to the French Academy in 1671.

We must now turn to his role as an assiduous member of the Academy. We can read his somewhat modest and strained speech of acceptance to the assembled body of writers: "When I consider the honor bestowed upon me in becoming a member of this illustrious body, and when at the same time I think how little I deserve this distinction, I do not know which is greater, my joy or my confusion."[11] In translating the passage we have not tried to modernize it too much, if only to emphasize how tritely modern the tone and thought of Perrault were. These same words could easily be uttered by a twentieth-century executive thanking the members of the board of directors for electing him their president, or an eighteen-year-old elected to a club. Perrault became a member of the Academy at the urging of Colbert and with the approval of the king which was always needed for the submission of any name as candidate. The other academicians knew that Perrault would talk about the meetings of the Academy to Colbert.

Perrault had been elected to that body at a delicate moment of its life. The Academy had been somewhat dormant for the previous few years. Now the king himself became the official protector or sponsor of the Academy; he gave it new, luxuriously appointed rooms in the Louvre. The director, the archbishop of Paris, Harlay de Chanvallon, was too busy to attend most of the meetings, and so the assembly elected Perrault as their acting director, or *Chancelier*, in 1671. He was reelected again the following year, a sure sign his colleagues liked him. His contributions and activities are well documented. Quite a few of his innovations became traditions and endure to this day. The *Discours de réception* of newly elected members became a public event and the occasion for presenting a polished piece of work, eventually to be published. The country became aware and proud of this institution. Furthermore, in an effort to avoid too much political polarization, Perrault introduced secret ballots in the election of new members.

Perrault was a born attender of meetings, what we would today call an excellent committeeman. He knew how to make others work as a group, and he had "strong executive abilities." Here are a few of his words, indirectly quoted through the official records of the Academy: "M. Perrault ... urged them, with a few words, but full of energy, to work more arduously and with more punctuality, emphatically insisting that the honor bestowed upon them today should build up their courage and double their zeal, so that they could prove to the public that they were not entirely unworthy of the favor they received from the most noble king in the world."[12] With such a charge, the forty "immortals" buckled down to work. The most urgent task was that of the dictionary of the French language, known as the *Dictionnaire de l'Académie*. Perrault joined the company of writers in 1671, and by assiduously urging on his fellow writers and not sparing his own efforts—thanks to the rivalry of another private dictionary enterprise by Furetière—twenty years later, in 1694, the first edition of the *Dictionnaire* appeared.

Another innovation of Perrault, or of both Perrault and Colbert, was that of the *jetons,* or tokens. Each time a member attended a meeting he would collect a token, redeemable for a modest sum of money. Surprisingly enough, these tokens improved attendance spectacularly.

The activity of Perrault was unceasing. He informed the public of various prizes for achievements in poetry or for speeches, what was then called *éloquence.* He often served as speaker of the house when the king visited the Academy, and, most importantly, he served as a personable and informed intermediary between the government and the Academy. There may have been other academicians of greater renown than Perrault, but none worked harder than he, none marked the Academy so profoundly in its early formative years. After all, the Academy had been founded just thirty-seven years before he was elected.

His activity as a public servant coincided with his work as an academician. There is no doubt that his literary production slackened somewhat. However, in the collection of his poems and speeches printed in the *Recueil de divers ouvrages en prose et en vers* (printed in 1675; reprinted in 1676, with additions), we find a few interesting pieces. The "Labyrinthe de Versailles" [The Labyrinth of Versailles] is a short description of the Versailles gardens, decorated with an ensemble of fountains and sculptures designed to illustrate some thirty-eight selected fables of Aesop. Perrault, at the same time La Fontaine was publishing his *Fables,* was trying his hand too at the art of the fable. A description of each fountain is followed by a short poem of a gallant nature, witty and short. This structure is a prefiguration of the famous fairy tales. There is, first, a prose narrative and then a moral in verse. In fact, one of the fables is actually echoed in one of the fairy tales. In "Le Chat botté" [Puss in Boots] there is, as in fable 5, a cat hanging by his legs and feigning death, in order to catch rats. The verse moral is very short and worth quoting and analyzing: "The safest thing to do most of the time is to pull away / A Cat is a Cat, a Flirt is a Flirt."[13] These two lines are a good example of "Brevity is the soul of wit." Here Perrault is saying that mice had better stay away from cats, even if they seem dead, for they might spring to life. Then he makes a quick analogy between lovers as mice and coquettes or flirts as cats, suggesting that neither can change their nature, and that both can trap and "kill" anyone simply because it is their function in the scheme of Nature. But our explanation is too long. Perrault said it better: "Un Chat est un Chat. . . ."

The last piece of Perrault's *Recueil* is a defense of the opera in general and of Quinault's *Alceste* in particular. Literary opinion in France was then, and still is now, a question of cliques, and Quinault did not seem to be liked by the Boileau-Racine clique. Perrault belonged to another clique, that of the "older, *précieux*" poets. Yet, paradoxically, Perrault appreciated all that was modern at the time. The opera was a new genre, at least in France, and Perrault was enchanted by the huge display of moving scenery, the aerial movement of mythological figures and other theatrical tricks called *théâtre à machines*. Of course, he also appreciated the music and the singing. However, Boileau ridiculed the operas of Quinault, especially *Alceste,* on the pretext, among other objections, that Quinault did not follow closely enough his Greek model in the tragedy of Euripides. The main argument of the tragedy concerned the voluntary sacrifice of Alcestis who gave her life to save that of her husband Admette. In the end Hercules miraculously brought Alcestis back to life and returned her to her husband.

Perrault's defense is entitled "Critique de l'Opéra ou Examen de la tragédie intitulée Alceste ou le Triomphe d'Alcide" [Critique of the Opera or Discussion of the Tragedy of Alceste or the Triumph of Alcide]. The main arguments are presented in dialogue form between two characters, Aristippe and Cléon. The latter defends modern taste and judgment by boldly asserting that it is not necessary to know the precepts of Aristotle and

Horace in order to appreciate good plays, for "comedies [any works performed on stage] are created to please not only the learned, but all the ... people, and a stage production has fulfilled its role if it has brought pleasure to its audience."[14]

Perrault was to be criticized again, this time not by Boileau, but by Racine, and not for claiming that the opera of Quinault was beautiful and pleasing but for having made a mistake in quoting Euripides. The whole incident may seem ridiculous to us now. Racine had written his criticism in the preface of his tragedy *Iphigénie*. What is at stake here is more than a vain quarrel of erudition. It is a question of attitudes. Perrault was simply not reverent toward the authors of antiquity. His answer to Racine (published by Paul Bonnefon) is little known and appeared in his "Lettre à M. Charpentier, de l'Académie française, sur la préface de l'Iphigénie de M. Racine" [Letter to Mr. Charpentier of the French Academy, concerning Racine's preface to his Iphigenia]. Here are two characteristic ideas of Perrault: "You may think, sir, that I am a *libertin* ["freethinker"] who lacks respect for these great men who are our masters ... but I am not convinced that their works are divine. ... We have today authors whom I admire as much as the ancients, such as M. Racine, and five or six others with him, if he does not mind."[15]

Perrault certainly had the courage of his convictions. He formed his tastes in independence and bowed to no author, modern or ancient. His activities as a member of the Academy were to give that body a decisive push in the right direction.

CHAPTER 3

The Polemicist and Apologist of his Age

I The Great Quarrel Begins

IN January, 1687, Louis XIV had recovered from a serious sur-
gical operation, a fistula. In those days it was a dangerous
(no antiseptics) and painful (no anesthesia) ordeal. That he
survived is a tribute to his vitality. On the twenty-sixth of
that month the Academy was meeting, in full regalia, to celebrate
publicly the king's return to health. There were prayers and
various speeches. Then came the turn of Abbé Lavau, who
read a long poem of Charles Perrault, *Le Siècle de Louis le
Grand* [The Century of Louis the Great], which was to set
off one of the most celebrated controversies in literary history.
It begins:

> Beautiful Antiquity has always been venerable,
> But n'er did I believe it to be adorable,
> The Ancients I see without bending my knee,
> They are grand, 'tis true, but men like you and me:
> And without fear of injustice one can compare,
> Louis' great century to Augustus' so fair.[1]

It was a defiant beginning. At once a great debate broke out in
the Academy. Perrault made the mistake, however, of ridicul-
ing Plato: "Plato, who was divine in the days of our ancestors /
Is beginning to sound sometimes boring. . . ."[2] This was enough
to anger Boileau, who was at pains to remain silent. The poem
is too lengthy (532 lines), not always euphonious, too didactic,
and filled with an excess of praise for the king. What mattered
then, and what matters now, is Perrault's thesis: the superiority
of modern knowledge, especially in seventeenth-century France,

43

over that of the Greeks and Romans. Everything Perrault wrote about the progress of the sciences rings true. The seventeenth century was an age of great scientific achievement in astronomy, optics, physics, and medicine, in particular. About astronomy he writes: "In the uncertain enclosure of this vast universe, / A thousand new voices have been discovered, / And new suns, when night spreads forth its veil, / Equal henceforth the stars' great numbers."[3] And about optics, in praise of the new power of the modern telescope, these verses: "Oh Heavens! since the day an incomparable art / Found the happy secret of this admirable glass, / By which nothing on Earth or high in the Heavens, / However far away, is ever too far from our eyes."[4]

When Perrault praises the painters and sculptors of his age, he does not quite hit the mark. He is also somewhat mistaken in his thinking that the French painters of his century were better than those of the Italian Renaissance. His qualified praise of Raphael and other painters of that period, whom he considered inferior in achievement to the French painters [the mediocre Le Brun, in particular], has not been ratified by our own century's art historians. We find it odd that he did not mention the remarkable colors and light effects of Georges de la Tour, the elegiac qualities of Poussin, nor the magnificent landscapes of Le Lorrain, or the realistic portraits of the Brothers Le Nain and Philippe de Champaigne.

As we come to poetry and literature, we can praise Perrault's appreciation of Molière and Corneille while we regret his not mentioning the names of La Fontaine, Racine, or Boileau. We can, moreover, lament his overpraise of mostly second-rate poets: Régnier, Mainard, Gombauld, Malherbe, Godeau, Racan. In this cascade of names, the specialists will recognize only *précieux* poets and of these, only one, Malherbe, remains admired. Why did Perrault fail to mention Boileau and Racine among the Moderns? Such omission might explain their anger toward him. Boileau was incensed, shouting that such a poem brought shame on the Academy and should be stopped at once, but his colleagues persuaded him to silence himself. The reading of the poem continued, with Perrault proclaiming, in some of the last verses, his century as the zenith of European accomplishment:

Nature has forever renewed itself,
Its being is immutable; and that simple force
By which all is produced, has not been exhausted. . . .
By that same hand, infinite forces
Bring forth in all centuries like geniuses.[5]

The idea developed above by Perrault is that Nature was not
worn out after producing the geniuses of antiquity. Nature or
Providence, at all times, can produce great artists; the forces of
Nature are infinitely born anew. It is an evolutionary concept
of nature, a continuous process: anyone can accept, it seems,
the renewing power of Nature (although we "Moderns" of the
last half of the twentieth century have second thoughts about
such things as the danger of radioactivity and, in general,
the future of life on earth). The poem ended, as expected, with
the familiar eulogy of the king.

There is something a bit combative in the tone of the poem.
It seems that Perrault was trying to reach not the restricted
audience of the Academy, but rather the public at large. France
is the country of intellectual polemics, and literary questions
have a way of polarizing themselves into political positions.
In our own century, during the late 1940s and early 1950s there
was the "existentialist quarrel" which opposed the "neoMarx-
ist existentialist Sartre" and the "neoclassic humanist Camus."
All intellectual France took sides and watched. One had to be
for Sartre and therefore against Camus, and vice versa, in the
same way that one had to be on the left, or the right, politically.
Three hundred years ago Perrault could have been on the left,
a "liberal-modern," and Boileau on the right, "conservative-
traditional-classical." And the insults, disguised as elegant epigrams, or as prefaces to this or that book, or simply as published letters, flowed from both sides. With the detachment of
humorous insight, the Quarrel crossed the channel and, in
English literary history, became known as the Battle of the
Ancients and the Moderns, summoning visions of aged scholars
throwing books at each other, entrenched behind walls of dusty
tomes. In its more "serious" context the famous Battle meant a
conflict between a positivistic view of science and a traditional
and somewhat narrow Christian outlook.

Charles Perrault did not expect to become the chief of a party, even a literary one. But his poem brought him much applause, and he felt impelled by his friends, as much as by conviction, to continue the fight. To reach the larger audience he dreamed of, he switched from poetry to prose, and we are grateful he did, for his prose reads so much more easily than his poetry.

The upshot of this brouhaha in the Academy was that Perrault's poem was not taken seriously by certain of his colleagues, especially Racine, who thought it was, indeed, a joke. As Perrault explains in the final paragraph of his *Mémoires*: "... I was annoyed that they did not believe or at least did not pretend to believe that I had spoken seriously, so much so that I resolved to say seriously in prose what I had said in verse, and to say it in such a way as to cause no doubt about my true feelings in the matter."[6] As we see from his own words, he turned to prose to make his point more emphatically in order to reach a wider readership. The result of this effort was the four volumes of the *Parallèle des Anciens et des Modernes*.

II *Champion of the Moderns*

To our knowledge, the *Parallèle* has never been translated into English, or into any other language. These thick volumes have to be savored in French. Perrault adopted the form of the dialogue, which lends itself readily to discussion, and can present all subjects and all sides of a question. It is no longer a frequently used genre, except in the theater. However, in the eighteenth century, the dialogue was still a widely used form, the most famous example being Diderot's *Neveu de Rameau*. Perrault used the genre imaginatively; he created three interlocutors. There is the fiery and witty *Chevalier*, a man of the world, not too well educated or informed, a bit like a sophomore, possessing the point of view of a student, having been bored with the classics, and consequently a partisan of the moderns. Also a partisan of the moderns, or rather their defender, is the *Abbé*. He is witty, steady, extremely polite, and the mouthpiece of Perrault, as he himself admits in the preface of volume

2. The third character is the *Président*, a kind, timorous sort of person, a worshipper of the ancients, but a good listener to the argument of the moderns. Inspired perhaps by La Fontaine who had chosen the Versailles gardens for the setting of one of his works (*Les Amours de Psyché*, 1669), Perrault imagines that the three friends are visiting Versailles and, while admiring the gardens, discuss the issues debated in the book.

The four volumes of the *Parallèle*[7] must be detailed in their picturesquely long titles: (1) *Parallel of the Ancients and the Moderns ... Concerning the Arts and the Sciences, Dialogues ...* (1688), (2) *... Concerning Eloquence ...* (1690); (3) *... Concerning Poetry ...* (1692); (4) *... In which are treated Astronomy, Geography, Navigation, War, Philosophy, Music, Medicine ...* (1697). Perrault's style is lively throughout, his tone never heavy or pedantic. In the preface to the first volume we find this ironic remark concerning editions with notes and the scholar who considers the authors he treats as his own property: "One can appropriate any author that one reprints with notes, however useless these notes may be." In the same preface, the main thesis of volume 1 is clearly advanced: "I maintain that we have today a more perfect knowledge of all sciences than at any other period of the past." The idea in itself is obvious enough, and Perrault tries to illustrate it throughout the first volume of the dialogues. However, he tends to confuse posteriority with superiority, a kind of blind bias for progress. This is akin to the modern belief that "bigger is better."

The second dialogue of this volume is devoted to architecture, sculpture, and painting, which Perrault knew well through his twenty years of association with Colbert. These were the plastic arts, his own domain in which he felt most at home to begin the whole debate. He deals with the subject as a kind of expert, rather than as a man of taste or as an artist. It cannot be said, nevertheless, that Perrault had an unerring sense of the beautiful, nor that he made a contribution to art history. His main argument was that French contemporary artists handled geometry, composition, anatomy, and the gradation of colors in a manner superior to that of the Greeks and Romans. He seems to confuse superior technique with great art. He forgets that a great technician in the art of perspective and painting can still paint perfectly dull pictures, such as the great "academic" painter, his friend Le Brun.

Insofar as architecture is concerned, he praises the monuments of Paris, particularly the Louvre, with which his brother was associated, over anything that exists in Rome or Athens. It is true that the Louvre, Versailles, and a few other seventeenth-century French buildings still make a rather grand impression, but when all is said and done, the architectural achievement of seventeenth-century France lies in the creation of unified ensembles of buildings in the neoclassical style. At this point it is necessary to account for what one might call the unconscious cultural inferiority complex of Perrault and his contemporaries. They were quite willing to claim that their art, their architecture, and their literature were superior to those of antiquity, but they still *imitated* Greek and Roman architecture, Greek and Roman tragedy and comedy, and Greek and Roman fables (Aesop or Phaedrus). They did not really invent *new* forms but recreated old forms in a new way. Thus the famous facade of the Louvre was an imitation of that of a Greek temple. The men of the seventeenth century seemed to say: "Look, we can build a Greek temple with Corinthian columns on an even more colossal scale than what you see in the Roman Forum or the Parthenon. And look how good our technology, our cranes, and our machinery are!"

It is curious that Perrault did not sense the inherent contradiction of his reasoning, and perhaps even more curious that he elevated the taste of his time as the exclusive rule in the fine arts, while implying that all is relative and that there is nothing absolute in the realm of taste, and that antiquity should not be taken as a model of perfection.

The second volume on eloquence is, in part, a running commentary on Plato, Aristotle, and Socrates in comparison with Descartes, Vaugelas, Voiture, and other philosophers and poets of the time. It must be understood that three hundred years ago there was much more oral delivery of literary works than today. In times that knew no electronic magnification of the human voice, the value of good oral expression was paramount. Perrault was concerned with beauty in oral expression in such genres as sermons, eulogies, and poetic discourse. He was concerned with method and logic as the typical operation of the human mind, what we call sentence structure today. He refers to a work which is very much of his time and very much in favor with linguists (Noam Chomsky, for one) and semiologists of the present century, entitled *La Logique ou l'Art de Penser* by Antoine Arnauld and Pierre Nicole, a work also known as the *Logique de Port-Royal*.[8] Influenced by this work, no doubt, Perrault goes further than the good doctors of Port-Royal and translates their systematic analyses into ingenious arguments or striking metaphors, such as comparing the composition of a persuasive speech to the ninepins of a bowling game.

The second volume of the *Parallèle* consists also of appendixes in which he gives examples of modern eloquence: the funeral orations of Turenne and the prince de Condé, by Bossuet, and some of the epistolary genre, with examples of letters by Balzac and Voiture. These are examples of the "elevated" and "pleasant" styles of seventeenth-century French literature, still read with profit and pleasure.

Finally, there is in this second volume of the *Parallèle* one of the most outstanding pages Perrault ever wrote, which contains a startling comparison between anatomy and psychology (the word itself did not exist at the time; he referred to it as *le coeur de l'homme* "the heart of man"). Just as the seventeenth century had discovered the secret of the circulation of the blood and functioning of the heart, so had French literature made new discoveries in the meanderings and motivations of the human soul. The tragedy, the novels, the works of the moralists (perhaps better translated today as psychologists) surpass the works of the ancient writers. Perrault concludes his argument, a bit bombastically, perhaps, but it carries its grain of truth, nevertheless: "By looking only at the tragedies of Corneille one would find no more searching and delicate thoughts on Ambition, Vengeance, and Jealousy, than one would find in all the works of antiquity" (2:293).

In the third volume, concerning poetry, Perrault spends much too much time decrying Homer. His favorite device is to find some passage of Homer which does not conform to the mores or good manners of the seventeenth century, and then suggest that he was a barbarian. Elsewhere he reproaches him for his extravagant comparisons. Then he chooses to discuss modern satire, and praises the burlesque verses of Boileau. He also defends his friend Quinault, the creator of so many popular operas at the time, but thoroughly unappreciated today.

Perrault does not mention Racine and Corneille as great modern poets. There are a few remarks on La Fontaine as a superior poet, and a few, very few, allusions to the famous *Fables*. But what Perrault writes has been confirmed by posterity. The particular genius of La Fontaine lies in his poetic humor and understanding of human character. *The Farmer and his Lord*, the fable chosen to illustrate the wit of La Fontaine, is aptly discussed.

Among other poets treated one finds Saint-Amant, the creator of the beautiful poem, *La Solitude*, which we still admire today for its harmony and its evocation of nature.

One curious idea of Perrault was to mention the *Devises*, that is, the inscriptions, in French or in Latin, carved on various monuments erected at the time. Of course, Perrault does not forget that while in the employ of Colbert, he himself wrote quite a few inscriptions. Most of them are of a symbolic nature. They are always short and concise. A great poet of the twentieth century, Paul Valéry, did not consider this exercise "beneath" him, and both the Museum of Modern Art and the Museum of Anthropology in Paris bear inscriptions authored by Valéry. Perrault remarks that such inscriptions are a legitimate form of poetry. They exhibit familiar poetic techniques, similes, comparisons, metaphors, and the use of allegory. With this discussion the dialogue closes.

Perrault's treatment of poetry falls short of our expectations. We would have liked to find more references to the great poets of the seventeenth century. It seems that Perrault had a whole dossier ready on the modern poets, but refused to make use of it, preferring to deprive himself of the pleasure of proving his point rather than continue to be at odds with so many brilliant men who disagreed with him. Perrault was always a gentleman in any argument and a man of impeccable manners.

The fourth volume containing the last two dialogues treats of the sciences in general. Nearly ten years had passed since the beginning of the quarrel. A sort of peace or reconciliation was more or less forced upon Perrault and Boileau. The tone of these last dialogues is less aggressive and much more urbane. Some of Perrault's arguments concerning the progress of modern science are expressed in an involuntarily comic manner, as when he feels sorry for men of antiquity, who were "incapacitated after forty, or fifty... because they could not read." Poor men, continues Perrault, "they did not enjoy the benefits of modern science, and could not wear corrective lenses, because these had not yet been invented" (4:37).

Perrault seems to be familiar with all the new techniques of medicine, surgery, pharmacy, and anatomy. He justly reproaches doctors of past centuries who relied on Latin treatises and never bothered to dissect human bodies to study the functioning of internal organs and their diseases. He is remarkably clear and concise in expounding scientific terms; at one point he even suggests a technique to construct hearing aids for the deaf (4:38).

Even though he seems to admire much in Descartes, he spends too much time criticizing him for some of his "mechanistic" explanations of animal physiology, particularly his idea that animals have no soul comparable to that of humans. Perrault certainly does not espouse the scientific, or methodical, doubt of Descartes, which he considers dangerous for the Christian faith. In this respect, Perrault seems not very modern and somewhat narrowly conservative.

Some of the best pages of this fourth volume are those concerned with phonology, music, astronomy, the accurate measurement of time—thanks to new pendulums and watches—and the new discoveries of chemistry. Concerning phonology, he justly remarks how euphonious the new mute E is to the ears of seventeenth-century man, what improvement it has brought to French poetry with such telling effect upon French versification. Similarly, he notices the richness of the new polyphonic music and shows himself thoroughly "modern," in the twentieth-century sense, when he writes about the wonderful effects of "well-placed dissonances" (4:9).

With respect to astronomy, he does, of course, praise the discoveries of Galileo, Tycho Brahe, Copernicus, and Huygens, brought about by the spectacular improvement of the telescope.

Amusingly, on the question of the rotation of the earth around the sun (4:31), he writes (in 1697) that the question is best left to the astronomers to decide. It is much to his credit that he dismisses astrology as a popular superstition and the "shame of centuries" (4:47).

Perrault, through his mouthpiece, patiently explains to his fellow interlocutors the wonders of the newly invented spiral springs for watches and the improved pendulums of Huygens, allowing for a previously unheard of exactness in the measurement of time.

We shall pass over what he says on the "improvement in the art of warfare," out of our own personal prejudice: there has always been, there will always be too much improvement in the art of killing men in warfare. On the other hand, Perrault has a sharp eye for all the new remedies brought from distant lands, and he singles out the then new "wonder drugs" of ipecac and quinine. These he discusses when he deals with the subject of modern chemistry. The dialogue ends, literally, with fireworks, for the youthful *Chevalier* reminds his interlocutors of the beautiful fireworks that took place a few years before, in the very Versailles gardens where they walk. They are told that their carriages are ready, and they depart for Paris.

This brief survey of the *Parallèle* does not account for what is essential in these spirited dialogues, and perhaps their most important feature—their style. That dialectical quality of the question-answer sequence, that constant intellectual searching, the frequent interruptions while the three characters are walking through the alleys and galleries of the Versailles gardens and palace, lend a certain heady lightheartedness to the entire work, rare in the literature of this period. For instance, there is the moment when the archmodernist *Chevalier* complains that the conversation has strayed away in "terrible digression," which prompts the answer of the *Abbé*: "What do you expect? Conversation cannot be really pleasant unless it flies a bit above the ground" (4:230).

Here and there, the style achieves a kind of striking power, while showing Perrault's acute insight: for example, when he refers to the Cartesian doubt as a philosophical "tool" (4:196), the "sommersault of Descartes" (*le saut périlleux*). Such a style is somewhat unexpected, as it combines acrobatics with philosophy. Most of the time, Perrault uses a wide variety of words from an encyclopedic range of references. We find here no clear frontier between literature, philosophy, the fine arts, and sciences: rather a curious mélange of all these. A recent reprint of the *Parallèle* (1964), under the editorship of the German scholar H. R. Jauss, includes an index of persons and subjects which not only facilitates consultation, but also reveals the importance of the idea of progress, among other topics, throughout the five dialogues.[9]

Perrault's insights notwithstanding, we should bear in mind that neither he and his compeers, nor Boileau and his, really understood very well what they were discussing. Their personal biases and passions did obfuscate somewhat their vision of the issues at hand. While we now appreciate more justly *all* authors or *all* periods, this was not then the case. In the Jauss edition of the *Parallèle* the following passage by a critic of the celebrated quarrel, writing in 1761, is worth quoting: "The partisans of the Ancients and the Moderns were attacking each other; and I would compare their quarrel to the battle between the Greeks and the Trojans at the siege of Troy. They were fighting in the dark of night, without knowing who they were, without knowing where they were going, nor what they were looking for. Indeed, didn't our contestants discuss these questions without knowledge of the Greek language, without fixed rules of poetic practice, and without any respect or references to the specific mores of the centuries concerned or literary history?"[10]

These dialogues are the expression of a thoroughly free mind, well disengaged from most of the current prejudice of his days. Many of his ideas are now commonplace, especially those concerning scientific progress since the Renaissance. Perrault was never pedantic, always courteous, and in many ways a precursor of feminist causes, since he insisted that women be always informed of all ideas and not treated differently from men. He was always proud to have women on his side of any argument.

All we have said so far on the general qualities of the *Parallèle* points to an obvious conclusion: Perrault was not only the precursor, but already a *philosophe*, of the Age of Enlightenment.

We can understand why in the following century D'Alembert
wrote such a vibrant *éloge* of him, why Voltaire and Diderot
admired him.

III   *Of Women and Illustrious Men*

Apart from the fairy tales, the only work of Perrault that has
been translated into English is the *Apologie des Femmes* (1694).
The English translation, *The Vindication of Wives*, appeared in
1954. Unfortunately, it does not include Perrault's fairly long
introduction. The *Apologie des Femmes* was written in answer
to the *Satire X* (1694) of Boileau, commonly known as his satire
on women. The satirist was a notorious misogynist who never
had shown any love for women. His poem seemed so violently
against women in general that Perrault felt obliged to take
their defense. He had been, we recall, a good and happily devoted husband and was at the time a not-so-young widower
raising three children, a typical "bon père de famille." In the
preface to his poem, Perrault takes Boileau to task for his violent attacks on womanhood. In a rather piquant passage of
his preface he tells Boileau that "according to your computation
of chaste women in Paris, we are almost all of us illegitimate
children . . . and you suggest that in a city that is comprised of
two hundred thousand women, there are only three virtuous
ones!"

What is most revealing to us about Perrault in this preface is
his somewhat strong attack on Boileau the satirist. A sentence
or two is worth quoting: "Instead of always crawling on the
ground, like a vulture who goes from one corpse to another, why
does he [Boileau] not rise above the earth like an eagle toward
the high and great subjects—Heaven, the earth, Hell, angels
and demons. . . ." Here Perrault clearly enjoins his rival to pursue subjects of a loftier nature and stop his attacks on women.

As for the body of the poem itself, it is a simple address of
a father to his son, advising him to marry as soon as possible.
It is a prosaic but honest defense of women. The following
verses tell of the evils of not caring for women, and it is supposed
to be a thinly veiled description of Boileau: "Who lives alone,
from women shut up tight / You'll find him filthy, mannerless,

and wild, / A boor in manner and in speech defiled."[11] This poem is not simply an episode in the Quarrel of the Ancients and the Moderns. It is the work in which Perrault has the courage to enlist himself as an admirer of women. His feelings were sincere, even if his insights on feminism were not as "modern" as they might have been, and certainly not equalitarian to the extent that today's standards of feminism would "affirm." It was a gallant stand, nevertheless, and it won many women over to his camp, for, in that age, it was rare that a writer would so strongly defend women.

The next most important work in the famous defense of the Moderns is a monumental achievement: *Les Hommes illustres* [Illustrious Men], two folio volumes, each with fifty portraits and fifty biographies of men of all professions who, according to Perrault, had glorified the seventeenth century.[12] It is thus a series of one hundred biographical essays, the first half appearing in 1696, and the second in 1700. While the selection of these illustrious men may seem arbitrary and capricious, we must recognize that practically every writer, artist, or statesman whom the judgment of centuries has considered outstanding is found in these two volumes. There is an apparent order in Perrault's selection, and in the preface of his first volume he explains his hierarchy of choice. In each volume there are, first, the men of the church, then the distinguished men of arms, followed by ministers or statesmen; then come philosophers and scientists; writers and poets; and finally, artists—including painters, sculptors, and engravers. Not without some humor (perhaps unconscious), Perrault remarks that they have all died. Therefore their social rank disappears, death being the great equalizer: "In spite of their illustriousness, their social rank does not matter, as soon as they are all dead" (vol. 1, preface). The quality of the prose in all these biographies (never more than two pages for each person) is outstanding. The style is at once clear, concise, powerful, and at times lyrical and poetic.

The very first biography is that of Richelieu. Everything is correct and corresponds uncannily to the judgment of posterity. A good example of Perrault's superior sense of style is the image concerning the enormous dike Richelieu had constructed for the siege of La Rochelle: "He tamed the sea" (1:1). Here are a few examples of Perrault's judgments and style. In his *éloge* of Marshal Turenne who commanded the royal armies in the difficult times of both civil and foreign wars, Perrault writes: "Divided France had to defend herself from the attacks of foreigners as well as from those of her children" (1:26).

In his biography of Colbert, Perrault praises the great minister for his keen understanding of the value of works of literature, which prompted him to encourage the king to subsidize writers: "...since he was convinced that the beautiful works of the human mind honor the State and the Prince more than the most beautiful buildings, he persuaded His Majesty [Louis XIV] to send stipends to men of letters, not only in France, but throughout Europe..." (1:37). Here Perrault is entirely accurate: at that time the king of France subsidized artists and scientists all over Europe, the equivalent of the Guggenheim, Ford, and Rockefeller foundations support today.

The biography of Descartes is a model of concision. In one paragraph he exposes all the principles of the celebrated *Method*, as well as Descartes's enthusiasm. This striking phrase comes to mind: "The study of Truth, his avocation and his joy..." (1:60).

This book is again the product of a free spirit, a statement of vigorous integrity of judgment, exhibiting a remarkable sense of synthesis. It is not easy to condense a whole life in just two pages, especially if this is the life of a creative genius such as Pascal, Racine, Corneille, La Fontaine, Molière, Poussin, or Saint Vincent de Paul. Perrault was ahead of his contemporaries for having sensed that his century was to become, in the eyes of posterity, the Classical Age of French civilization *par excellence*.

Whatever oversight or lacunae Perrault may be blamed for in his judgments in the *Parallèle*, they are partly compensated for later in the two volumes of *Les Hommes illustres*, in which we find praise of outstanding personages that he may have overlooked previously. For example, we do find mention of Mansart the architect, whose famous gables jut forth from the roofs of houses everywhere today, of Poussin, the dignified painter of classical motifs and mythological landscapes, and of the lesser-known François Chauveau, La Fontaine's engraver-illustrator. We might add Jacques Callot, the baroque illustrator, whose depictions of the horrors of the early seventeenth-century's campaigns brings to mind the works of a Goya or a Picasso on the same subject: war. With due deference to objectivity, we must add, however, that Perrault did forget—still—the Brothers Le Nain, Philippe de Champaigne, and Georges de La Tour.

In the area of literature, these biographical essays show Perrault the critic and witness of his time at his best. His concision enables us to appreciate, sometimes in a single sentence, the essential achievement of a given author, as we see in this comment on Honoré d'Urfe's celebrated *Astrée*: "This novel is not a pure novel; it is an enigmatic threading of the author's own principal adventures" (1:39). One cannot describe more simply what we call today a *roman à clef*. Perrault's statement about Corneille is that of a man who found himself constantly among the spectators of *Le Cid* or *Horace* or saw the great author himself on stage. Here is Perrault's firsthand impression: "Half the time spent during a play was given over to exclamations occurring from time to time during the most beautiful parts, and when by chance he [Corneille] appeared himself on the stage, the play over, the applause redoubled and did not stop until the author had retired from the stage, seemingly unable to withstand the weight of so much glory" (1:78).

In the same way, we appreciate the sense of immediacy which Perrault conveys to us in writing of the life and achievements of Blaise Pascal who, among other things, invented the first calculator, and a kind of "ancestor" of our computer: "At the age of nineteen, he invented and had made under his watchful care that admirable arithmetic machine with which one makes all sorts of computations, not only without pen or tokens, but without knowing any rule of arithmetic or without any fear of making a mistake"(1:65).

Perrault's statement on Molière exhibits, even more outstandingly, his artistic perceptiveness in capturing the quintessence of genius. Nor do we ever fail to recognize in Perrault's style the sense of direct historical perspective from someone who was present at the scene: "Until his time there had been wit and laughter in our Comedies, but he, Molière, added a great naiveté with images so vivid with the mores of his century,

and with Characters so well defined, that the productions
seemed to be less Comedies than the Truth itself, each one
recognizing himself in them and, even more so, his neighbor,
in whom one is more apt to find fault than in oneself" (1:79).
The viewer experienced unusual pleasure from Molière's plays,
and we can say even that they were very useful to many people.
Similarly, Perrault's talent for encapsulating in short paragraphs
the main contribution of an artist not only appears in the following passage but also anticipates our own twentieth-century
evaluation of Molière:

Combined in him are all the talents for a Comedian. He was such an
excellent Actor of Comedy, although quite mediocre in Tragedy, that
he was imitated only very imperfectly by those who performed his
roles after his death. He also understood admirably the art of cos-
tuming by giving to his characters a true authenticity, and he also had
the gift of distributing roles so well to his Actors and directing them so
perfectly, that they seemed to be less characters in a play than real
people. (1:80)

As for Racine, Perrault is to be praised for having written
an outstanding *éloge* of a man he had no reason to like, since
Racine had openly ridiculed and insulted him. One of Racine's
epigrams against Perrault invoked the Heavens to protect France
from his poetry. Comparative studies of Racine and Corneille
have abounded in French literary history for three hundred
years. Perrault, in this case, having seen the plays of both, once
again summarizes succinctly but accurately the achievement
of both in the following words: "The only thing which everyone has agreed upon is that they have brought great honor to
our Language and our Nation" (2:81).
    More importantly, it is all to Perrault's credit and political
courage that he incorporated in the *éloge* of Racine the Jansenist
poet's epitaph for burial at Port Royal, the Jansenist convent
and retreat house. That Perrault mentioned this epitaph at all
during a period of renewed persecution against the Jansenists
could be compared in some degree to persons speaking in favor
of religious tolerance during the height of Cromwellian rule in
England forty years before.
    The last biographical portrait that we shall discuss is that

of La Fontaine. As we read these pages, dense and full of insight on one of Perrault's most admired literary models, we cannot refrain from thinking that everything Perrault writes applies not only to the celebrated fabulist but also to the author of the *Mother Goose Tales* as well:

Works of incomparable charm . . . studied simplicity, witty naiveté [realism], and original humor which, never being aggressive, or cold, continually elicits the unexpected. Those delicate qualities, which can so easily degenerate into sarcasm and can cause impressions entirely contrary to the intentions of the author—pleased everyone, serious and foolish alike, high-born gentlemen and ladies as well as old men and children. Nobody has better deserved to be considered as original and first in his genre. Not only did he invent the kind of poetry which he practiced but also carried it to its ultimate perfection. (1:83)

We hope that in the above passage the reader has had no trouble recognizing Perrault himself in this *éloge*. For just as it is true that La Fontaine invented the literary fable, Perrault likewise invented the literary fairy tale.

There is hardly a biography or serious edition of Corneille, Racine, Molière, or Boileau, to name only these authors, that does not heavily depend on references from *Les Hommes illustres*. What we have said about this work barely scratches the first veins of a mine rich with significant information about the age of Louis XIV.

IV *The* Cabinet des Beaux Arts

In 1690 Perrault published a curious and lavishly illustrated volume, the *Cabinet des Beaux Arts* [The Study or Office of the Fine Arts].[13] The subtitle explains that the book is a collection of engravings, which are in turn copies of paintings representing the different fine arts as painted on a ceiling. The book also is a series of explanations or commentaries on the engravings and paintings. While the book begins with a dedication to a high official of the royal government, Louis Boucherat, chancellor of France, one has to search carefully for clues telling in whose house this luxuriously decorated ceiling could be found. The ceiling was that of Perrault's office in his house in Paris

at the time. Modesty prevented him from openly admitting that
his personal office was decorated so luxuriously. Yet the luxury
of such a ceiling is not in itself the most significant thing for us
as we look and read these pages with the perspective of the
twentieth century. The volume is interesting chiefly for two
reasons: for its repetition of the implied superiority of the
arts in the seventeenth century, and for its explanation of the
works of art themselves. Perrault's commentaries read like a
somewhat pedestrian course in fine arts.

The first thesis of the superiority of modern French art over
that of antiquity is familiar and need not be repeated. Perrault
provides us with a personally guided tour of a room in his residence. As we open the volume a full page engraving of a monumental door flanked by two life-size statues, one representing
Genius (on the left), the other, Work, beckons the viewer to
enter. The door is open, as we see a desk, a monumental clock,
paintings, busts, four tiers of bookshelves loaded with large
folio volumes. An inscription over the door reads: *Cabinet des
Beaux Arts* ("Cabinet or Office of the Fine Arts"). It is a formally emblematic setting, somewhat cold and classical: a representation of his personal office. Who, except an official in a
government office, would put an inscription over his office door
in his own home? What the two sculptures signify is easy to
understand. All artistic activity is the result of two necessary
powers surging inside of man: inspiration, personified by the
winged statue of genius, and work, personified by the statue of
a sculptor intently wielding his instruments.

Let us skip the first pages of the conventional dedicatory
letter and look at the text and the pictures. There is a general
explanation of the whole design, and detailed commentaries on
the eleven paintings or frescoes representing eloquence, poetry,
music, architecture, painting, sculpture, optics, mechanics (engineering), plus the mythological figures associated with the
arts and crafts, Apollo, Mercury, Minerva. The volume contains
forty-two large pages. It is not a printed text but an engraved text.
The words of the book were engraved on metal plates from
which the text was printed.

Perrault's aesthetics are dominated by the classically traditional notion of the arts as the mimetic representation of nature.

Decidedly the product of its age, this book provides us with fascinating and personal glimpses into the world view of a period long gone. A certain candor emerges from these pages. Here are a few examples. "All these fine arts," writes Perrault in his preface, "have been painted personified as attractive women whose beauty is related to their specific artistic bent, as much as the painters could convey." This is an artistic convention of Perrault's times, just as the rococo idea of naked cherubs performing as artists in various poses, such as playing musical instruments, holding brushes, or simply pointing, watching or listening. One of the most pleasing engravings is the one devoted to music. A rather Rubenesque brunette, one breast exposed, plays the lyre; around her a young girl plays the harpsichord, a seated boy plays the lute, another one holds a flute. Perrault writes: "The faces of the women representing Music and those of the children playing the lute, the flute and the harpsichord are rather lifelike portraits."[14] Gilbert Rouger, the editor of the Garnier edition of Perrault's tales, writes: "One could ask whether these portraits could not be those of his wife Marie Guichon and his daughter and his two eldest sons."[15] If they are, they would show a beautiful woman, in the bloom of her beauty, with her young children, many years before the publication (1690) of this work, for Marie Guichon died in 1678. By means of this painting, Perrault may have left us a hidden portrait to commemorate his wife and children.

A discussion of Perrault's conception of architecture will serve to summarize his view of the arts in his century. He considers architecture as a kind of encyclopedia for most other arts. Perrault explains that when man rose from rank animality, he started to build shelters that were comfortable and pleasant. This historical view of architecture states, for instance, that long before the Greeks built their famous structures, the magnificent temple of Solomon was an example of all the sound rules of architecture. He singles out three of these: solidity, function, and beauty. Among later examples he singles out, of course, the Louvre and Versailles. He believes that the famous eastern façade of the Louvre is the most beautiful in the world, admiring, in particular, the height of its coupled columns. A proud Frenchman, Perrault would not know, or even acknowledge, the great baroque splendor of Italy's and Germany's churches and palaces. Although he did not state it—posterity would do it for him—he was in a contradictory position. He was a Modern for his day, yet his century would one day pass for the century of classicism, and as such a century of the past. With the perspective of the twentieth century, we unavoidably have a different position.

CHAPTER 4

Perrault's Fairy Tales as Literature

I *Which Are the Fairy Tales of Perrault?*

WE have now reached the moment to present Perrault's most important contribution to world literature, his fairy tales, which have only been mentioned incidentally up to now. Let us first list them in the order of their publication. The list is impressive, if not large; and the reader will immediately recognize the familiar titles. There are eleven of them: *Griselidis* [Patient Griselda], published in 1691 for the first time, not really a fairy tale; *Les Souhaits ridicules* [the Ridiculous Wishes, or The Three Wishes], published in 1693; *Peau d'Ane* [Donkey-Skin], published in 1694; these three first works are known as the verse tales. They were followed in 1697 by the more famous prose tales, the *Histoires ou Contes du temps passé* [Histories or Tales of Past Times], familiar in both French and English as *Contes de Ma Mère l'Oye* [Tales of Mother Goose].

Such a popular title is generally associated in English-speaking countries with nursery rhymes rather than with fairy tales; nevertheless, the English expression is simply a translation of the French and did not cross the Channel until the first translation of Perrault's tales appeared in England in 1729.

The prose fairy tales are: "La Belle au bois dormant" [Sleeping Beauty], "Le Petit Chaperon rouge" [Little Red Riding Hood], "Barbe bleue" [Bluebeard], "Le Maître Chat ou le Chat botté" [The Master Cat or Puss in Boots], "Les Fées" [The Fairies], "Cendrillon ou la petite pantouffle de verre" [Cinderella or The Little Glass Slipper], "Riquet à la houppe" [Rickey with the Tuft], "La Petit Poucet" [Tom Thumb, or Hop O' My Thumb].

These stories were cast in enduring form by Charles Perrault long before the Brothers Grimm, in 1812, published their celebrated collection of folktales, in which most of the tales of Perrault appeared in German. They had crossed the Rhine through the first German translation of 1745, and through other oral channels.[1] This chapter and the next will treat of the fairy tales of Perrault at length, as their importance warrants. There will be presentations of the stories in a literary as well as in a sociohistorical context. Most importantly, we will also account for the special circumstances in which fairy tales became popular in seventeenth-century France.[2]

II   *What Are the Fairy Tales of Perrault?*

It will be useful to have for handy reference simple summaries of each of Perrault's tales. We have tried to write these summaries in a style that neither repeats the stories lifelessly nor reduces them to mere skeletal outlines. We added no extraneous commentaries. A remark is necessary on the subject of *Griselidis*; the story has no magical element. Nevertheless, Perrault included it in his collection of verse tales, considering it a *Nouvelle* (novella), a tale seemingly based on reality. But he considers the patience of Griselidis as so unusual in his time and day that he wrote in the dedication of the story, "That a Lady as patient / As the one I am praising here, / Would cause quite a surprise anywhere, / But in Paris would be considered a prodigy." Clearly, in his mind such a story tells of something long gone, a tale of passed times, as the very title of his collection of prose tales emphatically spells out.

We have added to our summaries a brief statement about each of the morals of the prose and verse tales, as they are rarely discussed in the criticism of Perrault published in English; furthermore, ignorance of their content amounts to a neglect of Perrault's own concept of his *Contes*. Our main intent in this section is to facilitate discussion by making our author's tales familiar. Of course, nothing replaces direct contact with the texts themselves. The salt, the wit of the language, in French or in English, cannot be savored in our summaries. And we should emphasize that these tales are among the shortest of fairy tales, a brevity they share with those of the Grimm Brothers.

A *Griselidis*

A certain prince who believed that women were faithless and deceitful vowed that he would never marry. His subjects, however, wished for an heir and urged him to wed. He replied that he would, only on the condition that his future wife be without pride or vanity, patient and obedient, and with no will of her own.

One day while hunting the prince strayed from the main hunting party and came upon the most beautiful young lady he had ever seen, a shepherdess watching over her sheep by the edge of a stream. He learned that she lived alone with her father and that Griselda was her name. At the palace he called his council and announced that he would not choose a wife from a foreign country but from among his own people and that he would not give her name until the day of the wedding.

Great was the excitement among the ladies of the land. Knowing that he was looking for a chaste and modest wife, they all took to styles more suitable to his taste, softening their voices, letting their hair fall loosely around them, and putting on high-necked dresses with long sleeves, so that only their little fingers showed. Great preparations were made for the wedding, and when the day arrived, the prince rode off on the path he usually took to go hunting, his courtiers following behind. At length he came to Griselda's hut where he asked her to marry him. She consented, but not before he made her swear that she would never go against his wishes.

Griselda was the perfect queen, and she gave birth to a beautiful daughter, whom she loved dearly. But the prince suspected her behavior and put her to the test. He ordered that her child be taken from her and brought up apart. He sent the child to a convent to be brought up by nuns. Fifteen years passed and she grew into a beautiful young lady, and fell in love with a great nobleman and wished to marry him. The prince, however, told Griselda that her daughter had died. Griselda was greatly grieved but her only thought was to comfort her husband. The prince was pleased with her but yet put her to the test once again by announcing publicly that he must remarry in order to provide an heir to the throne. He had chosen for wife the girl he had brought up in the convent. Griselda returned, in rags, to her hut, but shortly thereafter the prince called her back again to the palace to make ready the rooms for his new bride.

When the wedding guests arrived, the prince announced that he had only been putting his wife to the test. He then freed his daughter to marry the nobleman and promised to think only of his wife's happiness and to proclaim her virtues to the world. The marriage was celebrated and all eyes were on Griselda, whose praises were sung above all others.

And the people had great admiration for the prince, forgiving him his cruelty to his wife, for it had given rise to such a model of patience. Perrault did not publish a separate moral at the end of this story. Instead he expounded on a few ideas in the introductory dedicatory letter to an unknown and unnamed "Mademoiselle." He ironically insisted that patience "Is not a virtue of Parisian wives, / But through a long experience they have acquired the Knack / Of teaching it to their husbands."

B   *Peau D'Ane*

There once lived a king who was the happiest of monarchs and dearly loved by his people. The queen was a most beautiful and virtuous princess. The daughter was lovely and full of charm, so much so that having more children did not matter to them.

One of the king's most prized and most unusual possessions was a donkey who had the place of honor in his magnificent stables; for this donkey, instead of dropping manure onto the straw, deposited gold coins which were collected each morning. One day the queen took ill and died. The king was overcome with grief. Before she died, the queen had made the king promise that, should he wish to remarry, he would marry only a princess more beautiful than she. The king vowed he would never marry again, but time, and his councillors, convinced him that he must remarry in order to provide a male heir to the throne. He searched and searched throughout the kingdom but could not find a princess more beautiful than the queen to whom he had been married. He began to think that there was no more ravishing beauty than his own daughter, who was even more talented and delightful than her mother, and he decided to marry her. The young princess recoiled in horror at this thought and begged her father to reconsider. But the king was persistent and ordered her to make ready for the marriage.

For assistance the princess called upon her fairy godmother who suggested that she marry the king only if he could make for her a gown which was the color of the sky. The king, much flattered at her request, promptly produced a gown more beautiful even than the blue of the sky. A second gown was suggested by the fairy godmother, a gown the color of the moon, and a third, a gown as brilliant as the color of the sun. But the king had his tailors produce them as quickly as the first. So the fairy godmother proposed to put the king to the most terrible test of all: that he should sacrifice the skin of his gold-producing donkey if he truly wished to marry his daughter. To her dismay, the king dispatched the donkey in no time at all and delivered its skin to the princess. In desperation, she fled, with the donkey skin upon her back, as a disguise to a farm where she became a scullery maid. And so she became known as Donkey-Skin.

The only pleasure she had at the farm was on Sundays, when opening the trunk which her fairy godmother had magically transported for her, she would put on her beautiful gowns, one after the other, and admire herself in the mirror. One day a prince happened by and, having seen her through the keyhole of her cabin, fell madly in love with her, returned home to his palace, and stopped showing any interest in food or entertainment. He told his mother, the queen, that he would eat only a cake baked by Donkey-Skin, the ugly maid who looked after turkeys on a farm. The queen, thinking that her son's every whim, however irrational, must be satisfied, ordered that Donkey-Skin make a cake for the prince.

Donkey-Skin baked the cake, most willingly, as ordered, but in it hid her ring, hoping that the prince might discover it. The cake was brought back to the prince, who ate it most greedily, and almost choked on the ring. So delighted was he to find the ring that he kept it under his pillow. The prince did not want to displease his mother and father by marrying a peasant girl but, upon examining carefully the ring, they all agreed that it must

surely fit the finger of a high-born lady. The king and queen
acquiesced in the prince's request that he be allowed to marry
the girl whose finger fitted the ring.

Throngs of princesses, duchesses, marquises, and baronesses
arrived at the palace to try on the ring, but it would not fit the
finger of any of them. The prince asked that Donkey-Skin be
fetched so that she too might try on the ring. With shouts of
ridicule the prince's men led her to the palace, covered in her
donkey skin, underneath which, however, she had the foresight
to put on one of her beautiful gowns. The ring fit perfectly and
Donkey-Skin shed her ugly clothes to reveal a princess in all her
beauty.

The king and queen were delighted about the marriage of their
son to this beautiful princess. Great potentates from distant
countries were invited, including Donkey-Skin's father, who, for-
tunately, had forgotten his misguided love for his daughter and
was now very glad to be a happy parent at the wedding.

This story appeared framed by a dedication and by a statement
or moral of twenty-four lines of verse at the end. The dedication
to the marquise de Lambert contains the familiar defense of the
fairy tale: "Why marvel / If the most rational of men, / Often
tiring of insomnia, / Take pleasure in entertainment / Of ingeniously contrived day dreams / Tales of Ogres and fairies."
As for the final moral it was a reminder that the purpose of the
story is to:

> Teach children
> That they should suffer the worse of troubles
> Rather than fail in accomplishing their moral duties;
> That the righteous path can bring about much misfortune
> But eventually it crowns the virtuous with success.

The last verses of the moral have become well known in France.
"Donkey-Skin is difficult to believe, / But so long as our world
will bring forth children, / Mothers and grandmothers, / Her
story will be remembered."

C *Les Souhaits ridicules*

A woodcutter who wished to die because his life was so miserable was overheard by Jupiter, who took pity on him and prom-

ised to grant him any three wishes he made, whatever they might be. Overjoyed, he went home to his wife Fanchon and told her the good news. She told her husband they must think things over carefully and wait until morning to make their wishes. The husband, whose name was Blaise, agreed, had a good drink, stretched his legs in front of the fire and said, "I wish I had a nice big sausage to cook over this nice fire." A sausage appeared, snaking its way toward his wife. In anger Fanchon declared that only a stupid oaf could have made a wish like that. Her husband flew into a rage, saying, "To hell with this sausage! I wish it would stick to your nose!" And so it did.

Thinking of all the wondrous things he could wish in using his last wish, he asked Fanchon if she would prefer being a grand princess with a horrible nose, or whether she would rather remain a woodcutter's wife with the nose she had before. She preferred to be as she had been rather than an ugly queen.

And the woodcutter was, after all, only too glad to use his last wish to turn his wife back into her old self, which is what he did.

D "La Belle au bois dormant"

There was once a king and queen who, grateful for finally giving birth to their first child, a girl, celebrated with a magnificent christening ceremony. As was customary, all the fairies in the realm attended, including one, who through an oversight, had not been invited. Feeling deliberately slighted, she cast an evil spell on the young princess: that she would die by pricking her finger on a spindle. One of the good fairies, however, counteracted this spell and decreed that the princess, instead of dying, would fall into a deep slumber lasting one hundred years.

As predicted by the fairies, the princess grew into a beautiful and talented young lady. But one day, high in a garret at the top of the tower, she met an old lady spinning at her wheel. The evil fairy's wish came true, in part: she pricked her finger on the spindle but, instead of dying, she fell into a hundred years' sleep, as did the entire castle. At the end of a hundred years, a young prince, adventurous and wishing for love and glory, arrived at the castle as the trees and bushes parted magically for him. As he approached the bed of the sleeping princess, she awoke, the spell having been broken, and declared, "Is it you, dear prince? You have been long in coming!" The entire castle awoke too and the young couple were married in the castle chapel. Two children were born of this union, Dawn, a girl, and Day, a boy.

The prince, however, kept his marriage a secret from his mother and father, who were king and queen of the realm in which he lived, and especially from his mother, who was descended from a race of ogres who loved to eat little children. The king died shortly and the prince ascended to the throne, whereupon he proclaimed publicly his marriage to Sleeping Beauty. Consequently, Sleeping Beauty and her two children came to reside at the palace of the queen mother. A few months later the prince was obliged to go off to war. In his absence, ever jealous of Sleeping Beauty, the queen mother asked her chief steward to serve Dawn, her granddaughter, for dinner. The chief steward, who loved little Dawn dearly, slaughtered a young lamb in her place. The queen mother, pleased nevertheless with her dinner, ordered the same fate for her grandson, Day, but was tricked again in the same manner by her chief steward. She soon discovered the ruse, however, and ordered a huge vat filled with vipers, toads, and snakes of all sorts to be brought into the courtyard. Sleeping Beauty, her children, the chief steward, his wife, and their servant girl were all to be thrown into it. At the last moment, the king rode into the courtyard and the queen mother at once threw herself into the vat and was devoured forthwith. The prince, naturally grieved at the death of his mother, in time found ample consolation in his beautiful wife and children.

"La Belle au bois dormant" appeared in its final version with two morals. The first stressed with a touch of erotic humor the "modern" unlikelihood of a hundred years' sleep: "Now at this time of day, / Not one of the Sex we see / To sleep with such profound tranquillity." In the second moral Perrault characteristically expands on the same message, insisting on the "female sex's ardor in seeking marriage."

E   "Le Petit chaperon rouge"

Little Red Riding Hood, so called because of the red hood she wore everywhere, went off to visit her sick grandmother, bringing her flat cakes and a pot of butter. On the way she met the wolf, who wanted to eat her but dared not, because of woodcutters nearby. Instead, he asked her where she was going and suggested they see who could get there first. He took the shorter route, ran as fast as he could to grandmother's house and, having been let in, gobbled her up in no time at all. Little Red Riding Hood, chasing butterflies and gathering hazelnuts on the way, arrived later, and was let in by the wolf, who had gotten into grandmother's bed. The wolf told her to get undressed and get into bed too, which Little Red Riding Hood did, much amazed at the undressed state of her grandmother. When Little Red Riding Hood exclaimed to the wolf, "What big teeth you have!" the wolf replied, "They're to eat you up with!" And with those words he pounced upon Little Red Riding Hood and ate her up.

Perrault's moral clearly indicates the allegorical nature of his story; it is a tale symbolically recounting the seduction of a young child or woman, and he equates wolves with seducers: "I say the wolf, since not all wolves are of the same kind." The popularity of this tale and its erotic innuendoes probably account for the widespread use of the expression "wolf" as synonymous with seducer.

F "La Barbe bleue"

Bluebeard was a wealthy man but so ugly and frightful that he terrified women. No one wanted to marry him because he had already married several wives and nobody knew what had become of them. In time, one lady, eyeing eagerly his magnificent possessions, decided that his beard was not so blue after all and agreed to marry him. The marriage took place and soon thereafter Bluebeard was obliged to go away on a business venture. He instructed his wife to enjoy herself and to invite her friends over to his sumptuous castle but, at the same time, cautioned her never to open the door of the little room at the end of the long passage on the lower floor. Having given her the key, he departed. No sooner had he left than she invited her friends over to see her wonderful surroundings, but she was so curious about the little room that she left her guests and rushed to the forbidden door.

Upon entering she discovered a floor entirely covered with clotted blood and in this were mirrored the dead bodies of several women that hung along the walls: all of Bluebeard's wives, whom he had slain, one by one. The key to the little room was stained with blood but, try as she would, she could not wash it off. Bluebeard returned, asked for his keys, and noticed that the key to the little room was missing.

When his wife finally produced the key, Bluebeard realized her transgression and informed her she would be killed like his other wives. He made ready to behead her, but at the last moment her two soldier-brothers arrived and dispatched him with their swords. Bluebeard's wife subsequently inherited her former husband's wealth and married a worthy man who banished from her mind all memory of the evil days she had spent with Bluebeard.

There are two morals, the first blandly blaming curiosity as the cause of much trouble in the world, the second alluding to "Bluebeard" as a tale of past times and a story presenting a cruel husband, the like of which had disappeared.

G   "Le Maître chat ou le chat botté"

A certain miller died and bequeathed to his three sons all the earthly possessions he had. The youngest son received only a cat. Puss, overhearing his master's remarks of disappointment, assured his master of a comfortable life if only he would get him a pair of boots so that he could walk in the woods. Puss, being very clever, caught many a fine rabbit or partridge with his trap and presented these to the king as a gift from his master, the marquis de Carabas (a title he had invented for his master).

He laid further plans for his master by contriving an encounter of the king and his daughter with the marquis de Carabas while he was swimming in a nearby river. Robbers (said the cat) had stolen his master's clothes and he had nothing to wear. The king immediately provided him with a magnificent wardrobe and invited him to travel with him and his daughter in the royal carriage. They soon came upon peasants mowing in the fields who had been forced by Puss to declare that all the surrounding lands belonged to his master. The king was duly impressed by the great wealth of the marquis de Carabas.

Finally, Puss, preceding the royal carriage, came upon a rich ogre whom he tricked into a fateful metamorphosis, for the ogre could change himself into any kind of animal. He changed first into a lion and almost frightened Puss to death. And then, bullied into changing into a mouse, the ogre was promptly devoured by Puss. At that moment, the king's coach arrived at the ogre's castle, which Puss declared now as the property of his master, the marquis de Carabas.

At the king's request, his daughter and the marquis were married that same day. As for Puss, he never chased mice again except for amusement.

Perrault's two morals cynically extoll opportunism and good looks as inestimable assets for a young man's progress in the world: "Youth, a good face, a good air and good mien / . . . ways to win / The hearts of the fair, and gently inspire the flames of sweet passion, and tender desire."

H "Les Fées"

A widow with two daughters, one beautiful and kindly, the other arrogant and disagreeable, preferred the latter, for she was of the same temperament. The beautiful daughter was made to work in the kitchen from morning to night. One day when she was at the spring fetching water, an old lady of the village (in truth, a fairy) asked her for a drink, which the beautiful daughter promptly and cheerfully gave her. Grateful, the fairy bestowed a gift on his daughter: that with every word she uttered, there would fall from her mouth either a flower or a precious stone.

At home, when she spoke, she scattered diamonds right and left, and the mother was truly amazed. Greedily she urged the arrogant daughter, Fanchon, to do the same and sent her to the spring also. When the fairy, this time disguised as a princess, asked for a drink of water, the haughty Fanchon refused rudely and told the fairy to get the drink herself. Displeased, the fairy decreed that when Fanchon spoke, a snake or a toad would fall from her mouth. At home the mother was greatly angered at this and banished the good daughter from their home. Later, in the woods, she met the king's son, who fell in love with her, and they were married.

As for the other sister, she became so unbearable at home that her mother drove her out into the forest where, no one being of a mind to take her in, she lay down and died.

The two morals of the tale praise the youngsters who display good manners and *honnêteté* (a French word whose meaning was then roughly synonymous with courtesy).

I "Cendrillon ou La Petite pantoufle de verre"

A widower who had a beautiful and kindly daughter married for a second time a proud and haughty woman with two daughters who were as ill-tempered as their mother. They treated their stepsister most cruelly, making her do all the chores and forcing her to sleep in a garret at the top of the house while they lived in luxurious rooms. She was forced to sit among the cinders in the corner of the hearth and thus acquired the name of Cinderella.

The king's son decided to give a ball and invited persons of high state, including Cinderella's two stepsisters. For days they talked about nothing but the ball and made Cinderella assist them in their toilette and in their choice of dresses, which she did good-naturedly and with exquisite taste. When the two sisters left for the ball, Cinderella began to cry. She was soon comforted by her fairy godmother, who with her magic wand fashioned for her a coach from a pumpkin, horses from mice, a coachman from a whiskered rat, and six lackeys from six lizards. Her gown was of gold and silver, bedecked with jewels, and she had a pair of tiny slippers made of glass. Her fairy godmother imposed one condition: that she leave the ball before midnight.

At the ball everyone was awed by the beauty of the unknown princess, and the king's son fell in love with her. On the third night of the ball, he retrieved one of her glass slippers which, in her haste to leave before midnight, she had dropped. She arrived home late, and all the fine finery had disappeared except for the one glass slipper, which she kept.

A few days later, the king's son issued the proclamation that he would take for wife the woman whose foot fitted into the glass slipper which he had in his possession. All the ladies of the court tried to fit into the glass slipper, including Cinderella's stepsisters, who squeezed and squeezed, but could not make it fit. Then Cinderella, laughing gaily, cried out: "Let me see if it will not fit me." The sisters shrieked in ridicule, but the equerry who was trying on the slipper saw that she was very beautiful and let her try it on. The slipper fitted perfectly and all were astonished, but even more so when Cinderella drew out of her pocket the matching slipper and put it on, too.

At this the sisters fell down upon their knees before Cinderella and begged forgiveness for the ill-treatment they had given her. She pardoned them with all her heart. Cinderella and the prince were married and, for her sisters, she set aside apartments in the palace and married them to two fine gentlemen of the court.

"Cinderella's" two morals mention *grâce*—in its French connotation of innate elegance and graciousness—reinforced by propitious godmothers' upbringing. The importance of godfathers is also emphasized.

J "Riquet à la houppe"

A queen once gave birth to a most misshapen and ugly son. A fairy who was present at the birth consoled the mother by promising that her son would possess great intelligence and that he would be able one day to impart the same degree of intelligence to the one he loved best. His name was Rickey with the Tuft, because of the tuft of hair on his head.

Some years later there were born to a queen in a nearby kingdom two daughters, one very beautiful but stupid, the other intelligent but ugly. She became well-known for her wit and, gradually, became more popular than her beautiful sister. This deeply chagrined the beautiful princess, who went off into the wood one day to bemoan her misfortune. There she met Rickey with the Tuft, who had seen her portrait and was on his way to visit her from his father's kingdom. He proposed to ease her distress by telling her that he had the power of imparting his intelligence to the one he loved best and that she was, indeed, the one he loved best. The only condition was that she should marry him. She would have a year to decide. But she accepted immediately, promising to marry him a year from that day. At once she felt a change come over her and found that she was able to speak brilliantly on many subjects. She engaged in a lengthy argument with Rickey and, holding forth quite well, caused Rickey to fear that he had given her a greater part of his intelligence than he had retained for himself.

At court she amazed all with her newfound wit, overshadowing even her sister, who became quite saddened. Her father found her so intelligent that he consulted her on affairs of state and often held council in her apartments. Many asked for her hand in marriage, and she agreed to consider seriously a man who was extremely powerful, rich, witty, and handsome. To ponder her decision before giving it, she went for a walk in the wood, the very one in which she had met Rickey with the Tuft. There she came upon a kitchen full of cooks and scullions making ready for a great banquet, the marriage feast of Rickey of the Tuft. In a flash the princess remembered that it was a year to the very day since she had promised Rickey with the Tuft to marry him.

Rickey then appeared to claim her hand in marriage, but the princess replied that she had not yet made up her mind. A lively but erudite lovers' discussion ensued, most intelligently stated by both parties. Rickey won over the princess's hand by informing her that the same fairy who had bestowed upon him his wit also gave to the woman of his choice the power to bestow beauty upon the man she loved. The princess agreed to the marriage and instantly Rickey with the Tuft appeared to her as the most handsome, attractive, and graceful man she had ever laid eyes upon. As Rickey with the Tuft had foreseen, the royal marriage took place, as planned, the next day.

Love's "magical" power is once again extolled in the two morals: "Everything is beautiful in the object of our love. / Everyone we love has wit, intelligence, and great spirit."

K "Le Petit Poucet"

A woodcutter and his wife had seven children, the littlest of whom was called Tom Thumb, because at birth he was no bigger

than a person's thumb. During a bad year of famine, the mother
and father decided they could no longer support their children
and resolved to lead them into the forest to die. Tom Thumb,
who was the cleverest of the seven children, overheard their
conversation from under his father's stool. In the morning, he
rose early, went to the edge of a brook, and filled his pockets
with stones. The mother and father and their seven children
arrived the next day deep into the forest and, while the children were busy, the parents abandoned them and ran away home.
Tom Thumb led his brothers safely back home by the trail of
stones he had left to show the way. The parents, who had received some money meanwhile, were overjoyed beyond words
to see their children again.

But when poverty struck a second time, the mother and father
once again resolved to lose their children in the forest. Tom
Thumb resolved also to get his stones by the brook in the morning but found the door of the house doubly locked. It occurred to him then to use bread crumbs in place of stones. The
children were led away again and this time truly did get lost
because the trail of bread crumbs which Tom Thumb had left had
been eaten by the birds.

In the midst of fierce winds, heavy rain, and the howling of
wolves, the children made their way to a house in the forest
inhabited by an ogre who loved to eat little children. The ogre's
wife took pity on them and decided to hide them from her husband till morning. But the ogre smelled fresh flesh and discovered the children under the bed. He ordered his wife to fatten
them up, put them to bed, and he would have them for supper
the next day. Pleased with himself, the ogre proceeded to drink
a dozen more cups of wine than usual and it went somewhat to
his head.

The ogre had seven daughters who had all gone to bed early,
each wearing a golden crown on her head. On a separate bed slept Tom Thumb and his brothers. Tom Thumb,
fearful that the ogre might change his mind and eat them
earlier than expected, took the golden crowns from the heads of
the seven daughters and put them on his own and his brothers'
heads. Then he took his own and his brothers' sleeping caps and
put them on the heads of the ogre's daughters.

The ogre did change his mind and went upstairs to the chil-

dren's room to cut the throats of Tom Thumb and his brothers;
but he cut the throats of his daughters instead. Tom Thumb and
his brothers left the house and fled through the forest while the
ogre slept. When the ogre discovered his dreadful mistake in
the morning, he ordered his wife to fetch his seven-league boots
so that he might overtake Tom Thumb and his brothers. In his
pursuit, the ogre became weary and fell asleep on the very
rock which was hiding Tom Thumb and his brothers. Tom
Thumb took off the magical seven-league boots of the ogre and
put them on and raced back to the ogre's house, where he tricked
the ogre's wife into giving him all that the ogre possessed.
Laden with all the ogre's wealth, Tom Thumb repaired to his
father's house where he was received with great joy.

Another account—given by Perrault himself as another ending
—denies that Tom Thumb committed the theft from the ogre:
he went to work in the service of a nearby king, became very
wealthy, and returned to his father's house, where he was received with the greatest joy imaginable.

The one moral of seven lines expands on one topic: the hidden
talents and the sudden benefits that might accrue to a family
from its youngest, shortest, and most unnoticed child.

III *The Climate of the Fairy Tale*

In seventeenth-century France, there was much interest in
the allegorical, the mythological, the emblematic, and, of course,
the fairy tale. Much evidence survives concerning the telling of fairy tales in courtly circles. Here is an intimate
sidelight into the youth of Louis XIV, from Pierre de La Porte,
his personal valet since childhood: ". . . I was among the first
entrusted with sleeping in the room of his majesty . . . what
caused him the most chagrin was that I could not regale him
with the telling of fairy tales, which up to now had been told
to him before going to sleep by the ladies in charge of him."[3]
Just as interesting is this statement about the great minister of
state: "Monsieur Colbert, in his leisure hours, invited people to
tell him fairy tales, especially stories like that of Donkey-Skin.
What a pity that in those days Mesdames d'Aulnoy and Murat
[women authors of fairy tales] were not then occupied with their

fairies. He would have often received them."[4] Similarly, Mme. de Sévigné, the celebrated letter writer, in a letter to her daughter Madame de Grignan, writes on August 6, 1677: "Mme. de Coulanges [a relative] . . . was kind enough to retell us some of the tales with which ladies at Versailles are entertained . . . she told us of a green island in which a princess, the fairest of all, more beautiful than the day, was growing up; the fairies were showering their favors on her continuously . . . the tale lasts a good hour."[5] The impressive point of these examples is the emphasis on the *oral* telling of fairy tales, before any author, Perrault included, showed any inclination to commit them into print.

According to Gilbert Rouger, "long after his youth Louis XIV was still interested in listening to fairy tales, Versailles had its Mother Goose [teller of tales], wife of a state councillor, Mme. Le Camus de Melsons, a friend of Mlle L'Héritier [niece of Perrault]," who wrote the following lines to praise the woman who could entertain a king: "You whose lifelike tones / Found the way to entertain so many times / With your enchanting tales the most powerful of kings / Inimitable Mme Le Camus."[6] These lines can be dated 1695, through the date of publication of the work in which they appear. In that year, Perrault had already published three stories in verse, of which one was certainly a fairy tale, *Peau d'Ane*, that typical folktale, which he rewrote so delightfully. It was about that fairy tale that La Fontaine, Perrault's model as a writer, had written (in 1675): "If *Donkey-Skin* were told to me / I would enjoy it extremely, / They say the world is old: I believe it; nevertheless / We must still amuse it like a child."[7]

In the immediate vicinity of the king, Fénelon, the appointed teacher of the royal heir, thought of fairy tales in terms of their enjoyment and educational value. For him the animal fable, with its talking animals, and the fairy tale were kindred genres. In this respect there is a meeting of minds between Fénelon, La Fontaine, and Perrault. Fénelon had, in fact, written some twenty-seven stories (many of them fairy tales), around 1690. In that year there appeared the first literary fairy tale in French literature, the tale of "l'Isle de la Félicité" [The Island of Happiness] by Mme d'Aulnoy. The story, a rewriting of a very well known folktale, the "Land Where No One Dies," is to be found inside a novel entitled *Hypolite*.[8]

With all these "signs" of a taste for that peculiar art form, appealing at once to children and adults, partaking of mythology and popular traditions, it would have been surprising if Perrault, throughout his life a man ready to be "in the wind" or "at the scene" of all trends, had not picked up the scent, and had not started to produce his own fairy tales. And he had an imperative incentive, the education of his children, for whom he felt that entertainment and instruction went hand in hand.

IV   *Perrault, Boileau, and the Fairy Tales*

In one of his earlier works, the allegorical *Dialogue de l'Amour et de l'Amitié* (1661), Perrault had foreshadowed, by his delicate evocation of the "magical" power of love, the tone and the subject of his fairy tale "Riquet à la houppe." Similarly, in his "Labyrinthe de Versailles," he had created a structural anticipation of his fairy tales—little illustrated prose narratives or "fables" accompanied by verse commentaries or morals, some of which are curious foretellings of the morals in the tales. The following lines form a kind of introduction to the "Labyrinthe":

> Any wise man who knowingly enters
> The labyrinthine paths of love
> And wishes to travel through the whole of it,
> Must be cautious and sweet in his language,
> Gallant, clean in his appearance,
> And especially not behave like a wolf.
> Otherwise all the beauties of the fair sex
> Young, old, plain, or fair,
> Blond, brunettes, sweet, cruel
> Would throw themselves on him and
> Would gobble him up like owls.[9]

Another versified statement uses the same rhymes as the moral of the tale of "Little Red Riding Hood" to express the same message: "Beware of these sweet-talking young men [*douc-*

ereux], / They are a hundred times more dangerous [*dangereux*]."

Furthermore, Perrault alluded frequently to fairy tales in the text of his *Parallèle*. He felt that the popular but "modern" French fairy tales of Mother Goose were superior to the tales of antiquity, such as those of Apuleius (*The Golden Ass*) and many others. He found that French popular tales were "cleaner" than such stories from antiquity. He reproved their eroticism with his typical "Victorian" prudishness (2:126).

It is obvious that during those years of the writing of the *Parallèle* (1688–1697) his mind was occupied with the fairy tales, as well as with the Quarrel of the Ancients and the Moderns. For a man like Perrault, the hyperboles of Homer referring to Fate having her head in the clouds, or the horses of the gods making gigantic leaps, seemed somewhat more nonsensical than the "modern" imagination of the seven-league boots, which he praises in terms that sound somewhat Cartesian to the modern mind: "There is quite a bit of sense in that invention [of the seven-league boots], for children conceive of these as some kind of big stilts which ogres can use to cross long distances in less than no time" (3:120). Since the third *Parallèle* was published in 1692, this reference to the seven-league boots and ogres, practically the essential themes of "Le Petit Poucet," attests that this story was either known by Perrault or already in manuscript form at that date, fully five years before its publication in the famous collection of 1697. Interestingly enough, Perrault, in the same passage, felt the need to define the term "ogre," as if the expression was not too familiar at that date: "those cruel men, which are called Ogres, who smell fresh meat, and who eat little children. . . ."

But the most suggestive references to fairy tales are those in which Perrault writes of poetry and of the opera as imaginative expressions which partake of the supernatural, like the fairy tales. One of the passages deserves full quotation:

In an opera, everything must be extraordinary and supernatural. Nothing can be too fabulous in this kind of poetry; the old wives tales, like those of Cupid and Psyche, provide the most beautiful subjects and give more pleasure than the most complicated theater plots. . . . These kinds of fables . . . have a way of delighting all sorts of people, the greatest minds as well as those of the lower classes, the older men and women as well as children: these wonderful fictions, when they are artistically handled, entertain and put to sleep the powers of reason, even though they may be contradictory to it, and they can charm this reasoning mind far more than the most true-to-life works of art. (3:283)

What Perrault is developing here is an aesthetic theory of the fairy tale. He is stating, adroitly and convincingly, that there is a kind of aesthetic seduction in the enjoyment of the supernatural. He anticipates by three centuries notions that are quite familiar to men of our era. Wish-fulfillment seems to be the name of the game. But he is also stating that verisimilitude has little to do with reality. The fairy tale, even though it may be apparently nonsensical, has its own inner logic. He develops his ideas further when he states that the fairy tale need not be versified to be poetic, just as tragedies need not be written in verse to be tragic. There can be poems or fairy tales in prose, just as there can be tragedies or comedies in prose: "Since comedies written in prose are no less dramatic poems than comedies in verse, why could not the fantastic stories written in prose be poems like those written in verse? Verse is but an ornament in poetry, a great ornament which is not essential" (3:148). All of these references to the art of the fairy tale, or the poetry of the fabulous, once again suggest that Perrault had already begun to write fairy tales. However, the story now becomes murkily delicate: Perrault, as we have earlier noted, had an enemy in the person of Boileau, who thought that writing fairy tales was ridiculous.

Perrault first published *Griselidis* in 1691. This versified tale is close in tone and style to the sort of story La Fontaine could have written. The versified tale of *Les Souhaits ridicules* [The Ridiculous Wishes, 1693], is not very original either; it is but a flat adaptation of a fable La Fontaine had already treated, *Les Souhaits* [The Wishes]. The third verse narrative, *Peau d'Ane* (1694), is truly the first fairy tale Perrault ever published. Here we have the whole fairy tale paraphernalia of wonders: an all-powerful fairy godmother, a magical chest which follows Donkey-Skin wherever she goes, and a donkey whose litter is not manure but pure minted gold pieces (not an original invention by Perrault). This extraordinary tale was put on sale by the distinguished book-seller-printer Jérome Coignard at a time when both Perrault and Boileau were not on the best of terms. After the publication of *Peau d'Ane*, Boileau circulated the following satirical poem, which we translate and quote only in part:

> If you want to find the perfect model
> For the most boring of works
> Don't search the Heavens for it. . . .
> At the printer's Coignard, eaten through
> With worms, here is the incomparable
> Poet [Perrault]
> The inimitable author
> Of *Donkey-Skin* versified.[10]

In June, 1694, Boileau wrote to the great theologian Arnauld, who had agreed to mediate the quarrel between the two academicians, scathingly referring to "the tale of Donkey-Skin and the story of the woman with the sausage nose, put into verse by M. Perrault of the French Academy."[11]

It is true that in *The Ridiculous Wishes* the unfortunate peasant wife Fanchon has had wished upon her, magically and unfortunately, a sausage for a nose by her irate husband. To Boileau that kind of popular tale, fable, or fairy tale had no literary value whatsoever. He had not the slightest interest in popular tradition of any kind. The intellectual divorce between his type of mind and that of Perrault was almost absolute.

We can well understand why Perrault felt defensive about publishing his first volume of collected verse tales (1695) with a preface that took pains to explain that fairy tales were "legitimate." The next volume of eight prose tales appeared under the "authorship" of his son, Pierre Perrault d'Armancour, whose initials P. P. (Pierre Perrault) appear both in the manuscript of 1695 and in the first edition of 1697 at the end of the dedicatory letter to Elisabeth Charlotte d'Orleans, Louis XVI's niece. Gilbert Rouger is correct in stressing that Perrault took all possible precautions to ensure that the real author could deny he ever wrote the book.[12] After all, he must have said to himself, "this is child's play, nothing that Boileau could blame on the father. . . ."

V *Who Wrote the Mother Goose Tales of Perrault?*

Stated in such terms the question seems absurd. For the answer can only be: "Perrault wrote the tales of Perrault." The question is more subtle: yes, it is Perrault, but which one? The son or the father? While it is understood that the father may have thought it unwise to claim authorship for himself, and thus was glad to pretend that his son was the author, quite a few scholars have discussed seriously the possibility that the son may have been the author. Here is the case for the son.

Mlle L'Héritier, we recall, had printed a dedicatory letter of sorts to Mlle Perrault mentioning the good upbringing which Charles Perrault was bestowing on his children, who were all so intelligent and full of spirit. In that letter she mentioned the "tales which one of his young students has just put down on paper with such successful expression . . . please offer this story to your worthy brother . . . to be added to his pleasant collection of tales."[13] Such a statement seems to indicate clearly that Perrault's son had just written a collection of tales, in 1695, when Mlle L'Héritier's book was published. It may have been the very manuscript which the Pierpont Morgan Library acquired in 1953. However, since this manuscript is the work of a professional scribe, and therefore not in the hand of either the father or the son, we cannot find confirmation of authorship by its existence.

There is, however, another statement, in the story, "Marquise-Marquis de Banneville" (anonymous, *Mercure Galant*, September, 1696) which attributes without equivocation the text of "Sleeping Beauty" (published in that same magazine in February, 1696) to the son: "the Author . . . is the son of a Master [Perrault]. . . ." There does not seem to be anything ambiguous in these phrases. And the evidence so clearly points to the son that there seems to be no point in discussing the subject any further. But not all contemporaries were agreed that Pierre was the author, or the sole author.

The following dialogue from a book published in 1699, two years after the appearance in print of Perrault's tales, is suggestive:

. . . the best tales . . . are those which imitate most closely the style and simplicity of Nurses; and it is precisely for that reason that you seem fairly satisfied with those attributed to the son of a celebrated member of the Academy. . . . [Answers the other interlocutor] . . . one has to be an experienced writer to imitate convincingly their plain ignorance, and that is not anyone's gift; and no matter how much I admire the son of that member of the Academy, I find it hardly believable that the father did not have a hand in the writing of his book.[14]

The words "attributed to the son" seem to imply that at the time there was doubt or discussion about the question of authorship. The last words of the quotation suggest a collaboration; contemporaries found it quite plausible that the tales could have been written by the son, provided the father had helped him. Some critics have gone to great length to try to discern and unravel what might have been written by the father, and what by the son. Sainte-Beuve found the morals disruptive, because their refined and gallant tone differed so strikingly from the tales themselves. The conclusion was that only the father could have written them.[15] According to another critic, the father added many of the little digressions on love, the little parodies of manners, the remarks on feminine psychology, and the descriptions of interiors; other elements of the tales, such as the witty remarks, the love of the countryside, and the simplicity of the style would point to the son.[16]

The authorship question is not a puzzle that is easy to solve; quite a case can be made for the father as the author. Besides, the tales give the impression of an organic whole, a finished work of art, which rather suggests the product of but one mind, or the result of a very harmonious integration of many parts.

The son may well have helped the father, or vice versa. What we do know about the son did not, until recent years, amount to very much: the testimony of his collaboration, the date of birth (1678), and of his death (1700). When he died he was in the army. His death notice mentions that he had been a "lieutenant in the Regiment Dauphin. He was the son of Mr. Perrault . . . of whom we have many very esteemed works of poetry and erudition."[17]

Why was there no mention of the fairy tales in that death notice? The tales had already achieved quite a success, gone through many editions in France and Holland, and there was quite a vogue for published fairy tales at the time. The case could rest on these last shreds of evidence.

Since the recent publication of hitherto unknown documents from seventeenth-century archives new light has been shed on both the father and the son. We have already mentioned briefly the tragic affair of the involuntary homicide in which Pierre killed a young neighbor with his sword. Who started the quarrel, Pierre or the neighbor? We only know what a friend of Perrault wrote in a letter, "that his youngest son, who is only sixteen or seventeen years old, having drawn his sword against one of his neighbors of the same age, an only son, whom he killed while defending himself."[18]

The young man who was killed was the son of a woman named Marie Fourré, widow Caulle. There were many confrontations and actions in the courts between the father Perrault and the mother of the victim. Finally the affair was more or less settled (the documents available are not quite clear or conclusive) with the payment of an indemnity of two thousand seventy-nine French *livres* ("pounds") on April 15, 1698.

The reader may wonder what all this has to do with the question of authorship of the tales. According to the French critic Marc Soriano, this event had a profound significance in the life of Charles Perrault. He believes Pierre Perrault was a child prodigy, a fact which explains that he could have written the fairy tales. The father and the son became fast friends and collaborators. At this moment of his life the elder man was past the age of sixty-five. In his gifted son he had found an unconscious resonance going all the way back to the circumstances of his twin birth. His son became for him the substance (and no longer the unconscious and repressed shadow) of his long lost brother François who had come into the world a few hours before him and died at six months of age. The happiness of creation in a "twin situation" was then one sunny moment in the life of Charles Perrault. He had practically "fallen in love" with his son (at the time between seventeen and nineteen) whom he unconsciously confused with his lost twin. Suddenly, the "dream" was shattered by this tragic affair of involuntary homicide.[19]

Whether we accept the theory that Pierre Perrault was a child prodigy (or rather at seventeen an adolescent prodigy), or not, there is no doubt that the event must have been very painful, very disappointing for Charles Perrault. Three hundred years ago, as now, it is a tragic affair for a father to "rescue" a son involved in a homicide.

This twin situation is discovered practically everywhere in the fairy tales and other works of Perrault. Apparently our author was obsessed with the number two. It was part and parcel of his unconscious. It is impossible to discuss the son without being faced with the problems of the father. When all is said and done, the father is more important than anyone in the elaboration of the tales, even if we admit that the son played his part in the initial composition of the work.

There are quite a few contemporary statements pointing to Charles Perrault as the sole author. The Abbé Dubos regularly sent reports about the Paris literary scene to a common friend, the historian-critic Pierre Bayle, then exiled in Holland. The following extracts are in chronological order:

[September 23, 1696] The publisher [Barbin] is also printing the Tales of Mother Goose by Mr. Perrault. They are trifles with which he did amuse himself in the past in order to entertain his children. . . .

[March 1, 1697]. . . . Madame Daunoy [d'Aulnoy] is adding a second volume to the tales of Mother Goose of Monsieur Perrault. Our age has become quite childish concerning its taste in books; we need tales, fables, novels, and little stories. . . . Their authors are those who enrich booksellers and which are reprinted in Holland.

[August 19, 1697]. Monsieur Perrault sends his greetings, but he does not believe you. He says that you are wrong to think that he could believe your kind compliment because he was simple and naive enough to have written fairy tales.[20]

The three previous passages were not intended for publication: they were private letters in which one could feel free to say most anything. From the first one, dated September, 1696, it appears clearly that the Abbé Dubos unequivocally identified the elder Perrault as the author of the tales, almost as if he had just spoken to him and were reporting his own words: ". . . trifles with which he entertained his children. . . ." The second passage again attributes the tales to Charles, a few weeks after they had appeared in print (in January, 1697). As for the third passage, it is even more explicit in reporting the very words of our author: ". . . he does not believe you, . . . because . . . he wrote fairy tales. . . ."

The French word used in the third passage, which we trans- lated by two words "simple and naive," was *bonhomme.* There could well be a touch of humor in the use of that word (practically untranslatable in English); it denoted something like peasantlike simplicity, a certain naive credulity, and perhaps a little dose of senility, depending on the context in which it was used.

In the periodical *Mercure galant* (January, 1697) there is a long passage giving news of Perrault's forthcoming publications, the fourth volume of the *Parallèle,* the first of the *Hommes illustres,* and then, without transition, as if it was understood only too well that Perrault was the author, mention of the story of "Sleeping Beauty" (which had been published separately the year before), then the following paragraph concerning the fairy tales.

. . . a collection of tales which contains seven new ones, with that one ["Sleeping Beauty"]. Those who produce that kind of work are usually rather pleased if it is believed that they have invented them. As for him, he insists that one should know that he did nothing else than record them naively the way he heard them told in his child- hood. The connoisseurs maintain that they are all the more worthy for that fact and they must be considered as having for authors an infinite number of fathers, mothers, grandmothers, governesses, and great-grandfriends, who for more than a thousand years probably have added of their own, always piling up more agreeable circumstances, which did remain in the narrative, while anything that was not of a good inspiration fell into oblivion. They say that these are all original tales, genuine as old mountains, easy to remember, and whose moral is very clear, the two strongest signs of the goodness of a tale. Be that as it may, I am quite certain that they will greatly entertain you, and that you will find in them all the merits that such trifles can possess. To be found at Barbin's [the bookseller].

No name is mentioned, to be sure; however, who would not think of Charles Perrault? This long commentary on the antiquity of fairy tales is almost a modern definition of folklore, with its insistence on the "informants" as authentic sources. And yet there is this other insistence on the element of elaboration from each individual storyteller. The editor of the magazine could not have written such a passage: the ideas are Perrault's. Like a leitmotiv we find again the insistence on the pedagogical value of fairy tales told by parents, nurses, or relatives—as in the *Parallèle*, as in the preface to the verse tales edition of 1695—and again mention of the valuable morals in the fairy tales, while still maintaining that they are *bagatelles* ("trifles"). Such ideas will be repeated almost verbatim in the dedicatory letter of the 1697 edition. In that edition the issuance of the *privilège* to the son can easily be interpreted as a warning that the father would resent the tales being definitely attributed to him.

For nearly three hundred years scholars have debated the question: "father or son?" In our opinion, it is a vain question that can be answered: "both," but we will never accurately know what proportion each of the collaborators contributed the most. We tend to believe, on the strength of the numerous references in other works which we have already mentioned, that it must have been mostly Perrault. The well-known and respected twentieth-century novelist (and writer of tales) Marcel Aymé wrote an introduction to Perrault's tales in which he favors the father as author. Concerning the son, he writes: "I am not of that opinion. If you ask a boy—like this one certainly must have been—to write a story which he has heard told by his nurse, you will find not naiveté, but preciosities, affected expressions which will spoil the simplicity of the original narrative. I believe that it is more probable that the young Perrault, well trained and well formed by his father, tried to report faithfully. . . ."[21] To this opinion of Marcel Aymé we add our feeling that it must have been the father who revised both the text of the 1695 manuscript and that of the first edition of 1697. A further element of "proof" can be adduced from the death notice of the father. Perrault's obituary in the *Mercure galant* issue of May, 1703, is fairly explicit, although still allusive in implying authorship of the famous work: "The felicitous fiction in which Dawn and the little Day [names of the two children in "Sleeping Beauty"] are so ingeniously presented, and which appeared nine or ten years ago, has subsequently brought to birth all the fairy tales which have been published since that time."

Thus, when such an important writer as Perrault dies, the *Mercure galant* editor did state that he was talking about the author of "Sleeping Beauty" (and other tales), the author who had inspired the vogue of the fairy tale in the final years of the century. In our next chapter we will again discuss more evidence in favor of Charles Perrault.

Marcel Aymé referred to an oft-quoted passage of Mark Twain concerning the authorship of Shakespeare's plays, a statement which is fully applicable to the problem of authorship of Perrault's tales. In that spirit, we could say that the fairy tales of Perrault are not the work of the Perrault we may believe, but they are still the tales of Perrault, just as Mark Twain concluded that the theater of Shakespeare is not Shakespeare's, but the work of another author by the same name.[22]

VI *The Sources of Perrault's Tales*

The phrase "Mother Goose," is a direct translation of the French *Ma Mère l'Oye*. In designating fairy tales in the seventeenth century, it was common practice to say or write *Contes de Ma Mère l'Oye* [Tales of Mother Goose]. Mother Goose came to England—and thus into the English language—through the first translation of Perrault's *Tales* in 1729. The English edition reproduced the archetypal frontispiece of the first French edition of 1697, showing a peasant woman spinning and entertaining a group of three enthralled children sitting by the fireplace. On the wall a placard reads, for the first time in the language of Shakespeare, the translated title, *Mother Goose's Tales.*[23] Through that English translation, Mother Goose was beginning its diffusion outside of France: first German translation, 1746; first Dutch translation, 1747; first Italian translation, 1752; first Russian translation, 1768. Insofar as French editions are concerned, they number somewhere between five hundred and one thousand, and continue to appear regularly. The first American edition appeared in Haverhill, Massachusetts in 1794, followed by that of J. Rivington (1795), a bilingual, luxuriously illustrated edition.[24]

There are stories somewhat similar to those of Perrault which existed in Latin, German, Catalan, Italian, and French literature before 1697. They constitute the tradition of the *Mother Goose Tales* before Perrault.[25]

It is currently assumed that all of Perrault's tales came from folklore or popular tradition, and that all he had to do was to transcribe them from some peasant woman (presumably Mother Goose) and publish them. The usual sources of popular tales are the chapbooks, which the French call *livres de colportage*, or *Bibliothèque bleue.*[26]

Of the eleven stories that Perrault wrote, only one, *Griselidis*, can be found in chapbooks which were published before his stories.[27] Extensive research has not yet produced any other such trace. While it is true that many of these volumes of chapbooks contain Perrault's fairy tales, they are all *subsequent* to the publication of his stories, and are mere reprints of his text.

Even if we do not have earlier texts from popular tradition, we can be reasonably confident that most of the basic elements of what the folklorists call motifs existed long before his renditions of them. A motif is "the smallest element in a tale having a power to persist in tradition. In order to have this power it must have something unusual and striking about it."[28] As we examine these sources or analogues we will become more familiar with Perrault's tales.

Griselidis is not a fairy tale, but he included it in his collection of verse tales, in 1695, along with *Peau d'Ane* and *Les Souhaits ridicules*. *Griselidis* is not at all of Perrault's invention. It is a *nouvelle* (short story with a basis in reality) about a forlorn wife finally rewarded and exalted for her exemplary patience, almost a female Job. Boccaccio was the first to tell the story (*Decameron*, X, 10) in the mid-fourteenth century, to be followed in 1374 by Petrarch who wrote a Latin version, which probably inspired Chaucer's "The Clerk's Tale" in the *Canterbury Tales*. These versions were translated into French, and there were many versions throughout the centuries, eventually many chapbook versions. Thus, "the story of Griselda, abandoned by lettered men, comes down into the petty middle classes, even the lowly people. . . ."[29] Perrault knew Boccaccio's story and he researched other versions of the story before he wrote his own rendition. He carefully "pruned" whatever he did not consider proper in popular versions, for he found that "Griselda had been somewhat soiled [become a bit indecent] through the hands of the people."[30]

The tale of *Peau d'Ane* is also present in popular tradition long before Perrault. One of the essential motifs of this story is the flight of the heroine. She is trying to escape from the incestuous pursuit of her father, eventually hiding from him under the skin of a donkey (hence the name of the tale). Like the expression "Mother Goose Tales," the phrase "Donkey-Skin Stories" (*Contes de Peau d'Ane*) was synonymous with fairy tales. It is quite probable that Perrault knew many of the previous analogues of this story: the episode of Nerones in the anonymous fourteenth-century French novel *Perceforest* in which a princess hides under a goatskin; the "Doralice" story from the Italian Straparola (*Piacevoli Notti*, I, 4) many times translated into French; or "l'Orza" in the Neopolitan Giambattista Basile's *Cunto de li cunti overo Pentamerone* [The Tale of Tales, or Pentamerone, 1634–1636].[31]

Insofar as the last verse tale, *The Ridiculous Wishes*, is concerned, this story of the ill-spent first two wishes only corrected by the third wish reestablishing the initial poverty of the "wisher" goes back to the Middle Ages. It was even present in Oriental tradition.[32]

As we now turn to the more famous prose fairy tales, we can pursue their sources closely and in more detail, as we assume the reader knows most of these stories quite well from his youngest years.

In "Sleeping Beauty," the magical sleep motif is very old. The Greek Epimenides slept for fifty-seven years, and the Seven Sleepers of Ephesus were dormant for two hundred years. And there are many other examples. From Indian mythology comes the story of Surya Bai, whose finger was pricked by an ogre's claw, causing her to fall asleep and be awakened by a king. Similarly, in the *Volsunga Saga*, the German hero Sigurd discovers the Valkyrie Brunhilde asleep, surrounded by a wall of fire, and he frees her. However, Perrault's "Sleeping Beauty" seems closer to the following stories: the anonymous fourteenth-century Catalan versified narrative of "Frayre de Joy e Sor de Placer" [Brother of Joy and Sister of Pleasure];[33] the adventure of Troylus and Zellandine in the sixteenth-century novel *Perceforest*; the tale "Sun Moon and Talia" in Basile's *Pentamerone*.

The impressive difference between these stories and that of Perrault consists in his treatment of Sleeping Beauty's discovery by the prince. In each of these previous versions, the enchanted princess is raped during her sleep by her discoverer, becomes pregnant, and only after having delivered one or two of her offspring does she awaken. We find none of this in Perrault. We recall how he had decided that *Griselidis* had become somewhat "soiled" through popular tradition. He would "clean it up" according to the French classical tradition of *bienséances* ("decorum"). And he did the same for "Sleeping Beauty." He could not tell such a violent tale to either a courtly audience or a group of children. It is impossible to assume that he was ignorant of the earlier, coarser versions. The censoring, editing, and pen of the author are everywhere present in the *Tales of Mother Goose*.

The next story in the collection, "Le Petit Chaperon rouge" [Little Red Riding Hood], does seem to come from oral tradition, and we know of no literary version of this narrative before Perrault. Readers will no doubt compare the stark ending of Perrault's version with the happier final fate of the rescued Little Red Riding Hood in the Brothers Grimm's *Rotkäppchen*.

After "Le Petit chaperon rouge" comes "Barbe bleue." Perhaps Perrault intended the two most fearful stories of his collection to follow one another. We tend to believe that the tale of the cruel husband may well be an original invention of Perrault.

However, two elements come from earlier popular tradition: the motif of the forbidden chamber, and the magical key with the indelible spot of blood.

The last five stories of the collection all seem to owe something to earlier literary models. "Le Chat botté," the story of an animal providentially helpful to his master, is present in the tradition of many countries. The closest literary model Perrault may have known is that of the story of "Constantino Fortunato," from Staparola's *Piacevoli Notti*. The absence of the character of the ogre and a few differences in the plot notwithstanding, both stories seem patterned from one another. Basile, in "Gagliuso" (*Pentamerone*, II, 4) also retells "Le Chat botté," with one interesting plot difference at the end of the tale: the cat hurriedly leaves the house of his ungrateful master who wants to kill him. In Perrault, it will be recalled (in the last sentence of the story), the cat sits in the home of the master he helped to become a king, and "hunts mice only for pleasure and not out of necessity."

The story of "Cendrillon" [Cinderella] has a long tradition that antedates Perrault all the way back to Egyptian antiquity, if we consider the story of Queen Rhodopis losing her slipper as one of the earliest prototypes. Yet the name of the heroine dates from Basile's "Gatta Cenerentola" [The Cat Cinderella] as found in his *Pentamerone* (I, 6). The very word "Cenerentola" already evokes the sound of "Cendrillon" and "Cinderella." The word has an interesting etymology. It incorporates the two Latin words for "ashes" (*cinis*), and for "carry" or "remove" (*tollere*). Cinderella, sitting close to the ashes in the hearth, is thus the ash carrier or remover. Perrault in his text exploits the idea: when the persecuting sisters refer to Cinderella they call her "Cucendron" (Ash-ass, or Ash-bottom). The first English translation of 1729 also plays upon the analogies: the persecuted heroine is called "Cinder-breech."

The subtitle of the story refers to the celebrated glass slipper. Nonsensical and fragile as it may seem or sound, glass slipper it is in the first edition; and this is what Perrault meant. In the magic realm a glass slipper can certainly be unbreakable. The idea of it is unmistakably Perrault's, like the invention of the elegant boots for his master cat.

The last story of the *Contes*, "Le Petit Poucet" is sometimes confused with another tale of a diminutive hero, *Tom Thumbe* (1621). While it is true that this earlier story is close to Perrault's because of that similar motif, there are notable differences in plot and incidents. In particular, the seven-league boots so prominent in Perrault seem to be invented by our author. English and American readers of this book will appreciate that the different tale of *Tom Thumbe* is the only one somewhat close to Perrault's that can be traced with certainty in previous English tradition. Here is the full title of that tale: *The History of Tom Thumbe, the Little, for his Small Stature Surnamed, King Arthur's Dwarfe.*[34]

In "Les Fées" [The Fairies] and "Riquet à la houppe" [Rickey with the Tuft] we have two stories already printed before Perrault by two women authors he knew: his niece, Mlle L'Héritier, and Mlle Bernard. Mlle L'Heritier prefaced her collection of stories, *Oeuvres meslées* (1695), with a letter to Mlle Perrault, the daughter of our author, and offered her a story to be included in the *recueil* ("collection") which her brother Pierre was supposedly writing. That story was not accepted because it was too long, but another one, "Les Enchantements de l'Éloquence" [The Enchantments of Eloquence], although still too long, might have inspired Perrault.[35] It is the same typical fairy tale known to English and American children as that of "Diamonds and Toads," in which the fairies bestow on a civil young girl the gift of uttering a precious stone or flower with every word, and, on a rude girl, the curse of spewing out frogs or serpents. The main difference between the two stories is in their length: one hundred and thirty-one pages for Mlle L'Héritier, a mere eleven pages for Perrault. Here our author proves himself a master of concision.

VII *The Supernatural in Perrault*

Perrault wrote fairy tales in which, by definition, supernatural events occur; but this "supernaturalness" is not what is really supernatural. The supernatural in Perrault is the mood evoked by the magic of language. Because he was so influential, and therefore so imitated, much of what we can say about him also

applies to many other authors. But we must remember that he
was among the very first to articulate the language of the
supernatural in literature.

There is a sort of logic of the supernatural: in fairy tales,
by convention, the *tragic is abolished.* Thus the miller's son in
"Puss in Boots" receives the lowest portion of his father's
estate; by all odds of normal life, he should be a loser. Yet he
comes out a winner against all these adverse odds: a contradiction to the conditions of real life. In "Hop O' My Thumb," a
diminutive hero is confronted by the most frightening situa-
tions, yet he will come out on top, save his brothers, and make
his parents rich. In "Cinderella," according to the timeless rule
of the fairy tale, the poorest girl gets the prince. By our
acceptance of the world of the fairy tale we enter a new
realm where "wicked" every day reality is considered not only
invalid but unjust and therefore immoral. Let our heroes and
heroines win all the time. Perrault certainly understood this, as
we have already mentioned in our discussion of his preface to
the verse tales.

Consequently, no adventure of Perrault resembles those of
reality. André Jolles is right to write that the veritable basis of
the fairy tale is that in its unfolding "the wonderful is not
wonderful but is natural."[36] In legends, which differ from fairy
tales, the miracle, in terms of divine intervention, is the agent
which makes everything plausible and natural. In the fairy tale
the wonderful element, in a similar way, ensures not only its
plausibility, but also its verisimilitude, if within a psychological
realm of artistic or oneiric make-believe (wherein lies the difference from legends). What we wish is what we believe for
the moment, according to the time-honored principle of wish-
fulfillment. Thus we find it natural that the brothers of Blue
Beard's wife arrive just in the nick of time to rescue her from
death; similarly, it is only natural that the rags of Cinderella
become princely clothes. In a word, it happens because we
expect it. Anything which happens is not logical if it does not
happen through the wonderful agency of the magical.

How Perrault articulates this principle shows that he understands the naturalness expected of the genre. He does not bother

to give too many explanations, but those he gives contribute to make the fantastic acceptable in a typically logical and French way. When the whole palace awakens with Sleeping Beauty, *chacun songeait à faire sa charge* (each character was thinking about fulfilling his appointed office), as if everyone—after a hundred years' sleep—was carrying his or her genetic code to do this or that job (perhaps like ants or bees). But how could it be otherwise? The whole world of Sleeping Beauty would collapse like a castle of cards without all the palace's attendants. It is once again poetic ⸱suspension of disbelief which carries so strongly our conviction. Strangely enough, even the element of humor, which some critics interpret as a disruption, can also function to increase the convincingness of the narrative. So, "since [the palace officers] were not all in love, they were dying of hunger. . . ." Once again, how could it be otherwise? Significantly, Perrault suppressed a sentence from the first two versions of the story: "it had been quite a long time since they had eaten."

The "reality principle" of Perrault and of the fairy tale in general consists of removing that reality from the world of today, so that it happens "long ago and far away" in a dreamlike realm where we can become children again, and believe anything and everything. We are asked to suspend our own incredulity in accepting the supernatural: a subtle game of aesthetic complicity in which adult and child commune in the pleasure of the irrational made rational or natural. We have seen already how Perrault "rationalized" the invention of the seven-league boots by stating that children conceive of them as "big stilts."[37] He understood that an aesthetic principle was at work: "these well handled chimera [fairy tales] have a way of pleasing. . . ."[38] The realism of many descriptions is one of the facets of his art of the supernatural. For the realistic details of the supernatural adventure help seduce us into believing it. There are many passages in the *Mother Goose Tales* that "root" them in the sociotemporal context of the age of Louis XIV. Time and again critics have noticed a striking resemblance between the palace of Sleeping Beauty and that of the Sun King: courtyards paved with marble, huge halls of mirrors, concerts

of violins and oboes, menageries of animals, entourage of officers
for the service of the royal family. It seems nothing is missing.
The fairy tales of Perrault are complete worlds in themselves.

Yet the actualization of the supernatural is still dependent
on other factors, notably the evocation of feelings and the
liveliness of dialogues. It is not true that fairy tale heroes are
"cold as shadows,"[39] at least in the case of Perrault. Any reader
of his "Sleeping Beauty" can recall the trembling and admiration of the young prince upon the discovery of his enchanted
princess, the fear and horror of Bluebeard's wife, not to say
anything of the many moments of sadness throughout practically
every story. A particularly felicitous expression of feelings is
to be found in "Cinderella." After her sisters go to the ball and
leave her behind: "She followed them with her eyes as long
as she could, and when she had lost sight of them she began
to cry. Her godmother who saw her all in tears asked her what
was the matter. 'I wish I could, I wish I could.' . . . She was
crying so much that she could not finish. Her godmother, who
was a fairy, said to her: 'You wish you could go to the Ball,
is that it?' "[40] This is a clear evocation of childhood, with warm
and tender attention to the speech of a child.

The Cinderella of Perrault is vividly real and different from
other Cinderellas, which makes us think that perhaps she was
patterned after one of Perrault's children. She leaps out of
the page again, when having caught the excitement of the magical
game, she says to her godmother: "I'll go and see if there be
never a rat in the rattrap, we'll make a coachman out of him."[41]
The child playing with her godmother, finally provided with
the famous pumpkin carriage, has now become a regal person;
yet she had almost gone to the ball in rags: "Yes, but am I to
go like this in my ugly clothes?"[42] We do not need to summarize
the story; we know how the godmother's wand changed her
clothes into royal garments of gold and silver.

What captivates us in this rendition of an immortal story is
how suddenly the transformation of the crying waif into a
princess was effected: a case of sudden adolescence, or adult-
hood, for Cinderella did not have the education which had
been lavished on her sisters. How did she find time to learn
how to dance? The real magic of Cinderella is the magic of

growth, not the pumpkin coach. That pumpkin coach, so basic to the story, so well-known, is a pure invention of Perrault—a fact not clearly understood by one of the greatest interpreters of fairy tales, Bruno Bettelheim. He writes ironically: "Perrault's Cinderella, who goes to the ball in a carriage driven by six horses and attended by six footmen—as if the ball would take place at Louis XIV's Versailles."[43] But Bettelheim does not seem to realize that in the France of 1697 it is perfectly normal for a young lady to dream of going to the ball at Louis XIV's court. Indeed, why not? And where else? Critics and psychologists of German background, like Bettelheim, often tend to have an idealized version of the fairy tale as a "pure" folk form that must not be embellished by "literary" elaborations; as if it could be a literary elaboration, even for a peasant girl, to dream of being invited to the royal court.

In any case, the realism of Perrault's tales is rooted in the evocation of the royal surroundings of the period he himself knew, because this is how the drabness of his present day was compensated for in dreams of the splendor with which he had been associated. This dream clothed in reality partakes of the wonderful, just as in dreams or fantasies we need the realistic touches in order to make pass for plausible the odd, the strange, or the supernatural.

To come back to our subject: the evocation of the feelings of fairy tale characters. The feelings of fairy-tale characters correspond to the feelings of readers or listeners first within a given cultural context (France) and then outside of France, provided the tales are successfully transmitted abroad. The dialogues are ways in which characters "come alive" in various ways. Here is fear in Bluebeard: "Why is there blood on this key?" "I do not know at all," replied the poor woman, paler than death. "You do not know at all?" exclaimed Bluebeard; "I know well enough. You did enter the little room! Well, madam, enter you shall—you shall go and take your place among the ladies you have seen there."[44]

Everyone knows the dialogue between Little Red Riding and the wolf, and appreciates its atmosphere of mock-tragedy or mock-drama, with the questions leading, in crescendo levels of expectation, to the dreadful end. However, it is little known that this celebrated dialogue was first printed in Perrault's collection and may well be his own invention, an invention that has become a tradition, the property of the world. That Perrault was aware of the dramatically pleasant impact of this dialogue is obvious from a very interesting marginal note in the manuscript text of "Little Red Riding Hood." The note refers to the key words of the wolf's last reply: "It is to eat you with." The marginal note reads: "One says those words in a loud voice to frighten the child as if the wolf was going to eat her."[45] The words of this note should be interpreted as a playful, humorous aside from the adult Perrault himself. Such humor and playful drama is overinterpreted by Marc Soriano who writes that these words are an ethnographical indication.[46] Perhaps, but we prefer to believe that in his family Perrault used to say those words in such tones as a game, just as we remember that our own parents, on telling us this story, would instinctively raise their voices, and then burst out laughing, telling us that "there was no wolf,' and it was all a game, a story. . . ."

CHAPTER 5

Formal and Nonformal Elements
in the Fairy Tales

I *Of Style and Substance*

NOTHING is more difficult to define than style. We can use the following workable definition: a writer's choice and use of words in a definite sociocultural context in order to express his intent. Opinions concerning Perrault's style are contradictory: he is either "one of the greatest writers of the seventeenth century,"[1] a statement we fully endorse, or he is the collector of popular stories told in plain language by plain people,[2] a mere transcriber, not a creator.

The contradiction we have just sketched seems inescapable and we shall attempt to resolve it as best we can. In this chapter we will compare the manuscript and the final printed text of the tales, show how computer-aided analysis of Perrault's vocabulary has yielded interesting results; attempt to show how characteristic Perrault's style can be; and how his particular genius was translated into the English language. In the remainder of the chapter we will consider such aspects of Perrault's tales as their connection with folklore, and, finally, their profound moral and psychological significance. Were Perrault alive now he would probably be simultaneously pleased and surprised to read all of the criticism and thought lavished upon stories which he did not even clearly acknowledge as his own.

II *The Manuscript and the Final Text of the Mother Goose Tales*

The comparison between a manuscript and its final printed text is no mere inconsequential trifle of scholarly fussiness. It can

101

be a fascinating exercise in precision and an invaluable key to the inner mind of a writer as he wrote and revised his work. For well-known and influential texts, such as *Alice in Wonderland* and Perrault's stories, this exercise can be both revealing and entertaining.

All of Perrault's corrections show a stylist at work, aware of the significance of the right word in the right place. This is obvious from the very first pages, those of the dedicatory letter. This letter was important for the career of Perrault's son, Pierre, who was nineteen years old at the time. The dedication of a book to a royal personnage by the son of an academician is not without ulterior motive, for "Mademoiselle" could, in return for a flattering one, bestow some important official favor on the young man. Luxurious leather binding decorated with the royal arms of the house of Orléans, careful scribal handwriting throughout, and especially beautifully colored gouache illustrations make this "publication" unusually rich.

As we glance at both texts—the manuscript and the printed text in the first edition—we find differences of vocabulary which suggest rewriting by the more experienced father. Thus in the manuscript dedicatory letter we read that these stories reveal a very sensible moral "for those who listen to them." In the printed text we find the same words with only one exception: "those who *read* them." This is indeed the passage from the "oral text" to literature, the realm of reading. A few other additions elaborate on the personality of Mademoiselle, which could only have been thought of by Perrault—the father, an accomplished courtier—and not by his young son. While the manuscript simply praises Mademoiselle for a mind "which has the power to rise to great things and to stoop to small ones," the first edition adds another sentence: "one will not be surprised if the same princess, whom nature and education have familiarized with the loftiest subjects, should deign to find pleasure in trifles such as these [fairy tales]."[3]

In both "Barbe Bleue" and "Le Chat botté" we find additions to the manuscript text which again show the hand of a stylist at work. Everyone knows the passage in which the unfortunate wife finds the bodies of women killed by her husband when she opens the forbidden chamber. The manuscript simply tells us of "several dead women standing up and attached along the walls. She almost fainted with terror."[4] The printed text is much more explicit: "dead women hanging along the walls. (They were all the previous women which Bluebeard had married before and whose throats he had cut one after the other.) She nearly fainted with terror."[5]

Time and again we find more of those finishing touches. In "Le Petit Chaperon rouge" the young child is described as unaware "that it is not good to stop and listen to a wolf," but the final printed version reads: "she did not know that it is dangerous to stop and listen to a wolf."[6] The addition of "dangerous" reasserts the meaning much more effectively and contributes to the familiar suspense we ourselves may well remember from childhood.

A number of additions bring out humorous or gently satirical "pokes" at the characters. At the end of "Le Chat botté," although we are first told simply that the king's daughter "fell in love" with the handsome miller's son, we now find in the printed text: "the daughter of the king found him quite handsome and agreeable, and the count of Carabas only had to glance at her two or three times in a respectful and somewhat tender way to cause her to fall in love madly."[7]

Thanks to the manuscript, it is possible to observe the technique of Perrault at close range. Every generation has experienced a feeling of direct communication in reading or hearing the tales. They seem to have been always with us, as if we had dreamed them into existence. These stories, however, are the result of a writer's careful craftsmanship.

III *Of the Computer and Mother Goose*

The computer is one of the most modern techniques that can be used by critics for vocabulary analysis. The first thing that must be said is that the computer is essentially an adding machine that sorts out and counts words in a prodigiously rapid way, but it does *not* think. Man must do the thinking and evaluate the results "printed out" by the computer. A question lurks in the mind of every scholar attempting a statistical evaluation by computer: "Will I ever find the word or words most frequently used by this author? Will this or that expression finally reveal or betray his or her secret obsession?

It would be gratifying for us to say that we have found the secret obsessions of Perrault through the statistical analysis of his vocabulary. But the simple truth is that we are not sure that whatever revelations there are will be of a spectacular nature. However, some statistical findings from our computer-aided research are suggestive.[8]

While the total number of words used to write the eight prose tales is 18,320, the corresponding total for the three verse tales is 14,100. In *proportional* terms it would seem that for only three verse tales does Perrault's vocabulary seem quite as rich as that of the eight prose tales. In terms of different alphabetized vocabulary entries—what in computer jargon is called "word-types"—Perrault's prose language amounts to 2,676 headings, against 2,611 headings for the poetic entries. In other words, Perrault's vocabulary for prose comprises sixty-five more words than were used for poetry.

As we compare these statistics with those available for Perrault's contemporary, Racine, we find that the author of *Phèdre* and eleven other plays needed a total of five thousand words. Perrault's vocabulary—considering his much more modest output of only eleven tales—is roughly one half that of either Racine or Corneille. If we compare Perrault's poetic vocabulary to that of La Fontaine—a more logical choice for comparison than Racine—we find that Perrault's total of different terms (2,611) is once again roughly one half of the 6,354 words of the celebrated French writer of the *Fables*.[9]

Perrault's language, like that of La Fontaine, Corneille, Racine, or Molière, is striking in its economy of words, once again, classical. But the vocabulary of fairy tales—imaginative as it may be—cannot quite compare with that of tragedies written in verse form. What we can, and must, say is that the vocabulary of Parrault is not overly rich, like that of his fellow writers of the age of Louis XIV.

Now what about the frequencies and the obsessions? Let us first state that in all languages the most frequently used words are the "tool words"—"of," "to," "at," "he," "she," "that," "what"—which are necessary to construct sentences and which we give here in their English garb. The enormous frequency of these words does not in itself prove anything. The frequencies we are seeking are those of other words.

Some interesting conglomerations or constellations of frequencies of substantive words struck us. These we print in parentheses after each item in English and in French. The words "king," *roi* (69), "princess," *princesse* (53), "beautiful," *belle* (34), "queen," *reine* (34), certainly suggest an aristocratic climate. The fairy tale almost always evokes the life of those "happy few" at the top of the social scale of the Old Regime before the French Revolution. There is nothing "abnormal" in this finding of the computer: after all, why should the lower classes not dream of the life of kings and queens? The dream of the fairy tale is the dream of the higher social order of wealth and power where everything is possible. The concordance reveals that family words are rather frequent: "children," *enfants* (46), "mother," *mère* (30), "sister," *soeur* (32), "father," *père* (22), "brother," *frère* (20); one could consider as family-related two additional entries: "woman," *femme* (56) and "little," *petit* (53).

The constellations of frequencies in the verse tales are also interesting. The words "prince" (51), "love," *amour* (30), "heart," *coeur* (27), "day," *jour* (26), "young," *jeune* (21), "beautiful," *beau* (19), "sky" or "heaven," *ciel* (19), "spouse," *époux* (19), "time," *temps* (19), "all," *toute* (19), "at last" or "finally," *enfin* (18), "great" or "tall," *grand* (17), "gold," *or* (17), "eyes," *yeux* (17), "to speak," *dire* (16), "king," *roi* (16), "lord," *seigneur* (16), "beautiful," *belle* (15), "pain," *peine* (15) seem to suggest or hum some kind of poetic phrase or some passionate aria from a familiar opera.

Similarly, the verbs most frequently used in the prose tales can be suggestive. The forms "had" or "had been," *avait* (150), "was" or "there was," *était* (157), "he went" or "she went," *alla* (42), "they went," *allèrent* (20) can only suggest two ideas: first, the emphasis on the *past* tense, and second, the emphasis on *movement*, through the use of the verb *aller* ("to go") conjugated in so many forms.

The computer is a tool of research to be used judiciously. Overly anxious about the possibilities of spectacular revelations through a "scientific" method of investigation, a scholar might

in his maze of figures and statistics miss the forest while looking
for the lone tree. Insofar as we are concerned, we are glad that
the statistically revealed vocabulary of Perrault has proved to
be so basically simple. Were Perrault alive right now, and looking at our computer printout of his vocabulary, he might well
agree with our observations. He would not be surprised to
learn that his fairy tales tell of adventures of kings, queens,
princes, and princesses, families of parents and children as they
happened long ago in a fast-paced world filled with characters
often on the run.

IV   A Sense of Classical Style

All the features commonly associated with French classicism
are present in Perrault's stories: concision, precision, economy
of words, and multifaceted and powerful suggestiveness. What
we praise in Pascal, Racine, La Fontaine, or La Bruyère is also
present in Perrault's most famous work. Nearly everything he
wrote in prose during the last ten most productive years of his
life tends toward concision and simplicity. While he was publishing the fairy tales, he was also putting to press his *Hommes
illustres* (discussed above in chapter 3), in which he was sum-
marizing in neat, elegantly penned notices of one or two pages
the lives and works of a hundred distinguished Frenchmen of
his age. That style is also present with its often concise sense
of efficient formulation in the *Parallèle*, in the *Mémoire de ma
vie*, and in the "Pensées chrétiennes." All these works have a
stylistic kinship with the *Contes*.

As we turn to the tales we notice how rarely they are
encumbered by too many details or descriptions. We often find
a tendency toward condensation and concision, especially when
we find two states of a given text. In "La Belle au bois dormant"
Perrault deliberately eliminated the dialogues and digressions
so apparent in the first text of 1695 (published in the *Mercure
Galant*). While in the first (*Mercure* edition) there are two
pages of conversation between Sleeping Beauty and her prince
after he discovered her, we have nothing in the final text save
this transition: "They had been talking for four hours and yet
they had not succeeded in uttering one half of the things they

had to say to each other. Meanwhile the whole palace had awakened."[10] The two pages of dialogue suppressed were printed in the first version between the words "each other" and "Meanwhile the whole palace." We surmise that very few readers ever felt they "missed" the suppressed dialogue upon reading in French or in English the story of "Sleeping Beauty."

And we do find numerous remarks on style in the *Parallèle*; the following, in particular, we consider rather suggestive because of its analogy between literature and architecture: "It is true that, on the one hand, architects dishonor their buildings by a grand abundance of superfluous ornaments; it is the same in eloquence [literature] where an excess of brilliant turns of phrase and excessive affectation will mar its grandeur and majesty (2:165).

Let us glance back at the statement just quoted from the *Parallèle*: "mar the grandeur and majesty. . . ." What has this to do with the style of fairy tales? Simply the notion that a certain sense of grandeur, pomp and circumstance, formalness, logic, and appropriateness reigned supreme in the minds of Perrault and his contemporaries. There was a sense of style in everything they did and thought. It was then, as it is still now, a dominant cultural trait of the French. So much so that one English critic even wrote a book called *The Formal French*,[11] in which the bulk of his examples come from the age of Louis XIV. A beautiful, and today very relevant, example of this preoccupation with form and logic is Arnauld and Nicole's *Logique ou l'Art de penser*, which ran through five editions in three years. It was read and admired by Perrault, and, we believe, echoed with unconsciously harmonic resonances. When we read in the *Logique* this example illustrating a syllogism:

Divine law orders men to honor kings:
Louis XIV is King;
Divine law therefore orders us to honor Louis XIV,[12]

we cannot help thinking that this is precisely the kind of example Perrault would have thought of to illustrate a syllogism in "modern" terms. To our twentieth-century eyes this example for a syllogism might seem jarring. It is probably superfluous to state that it did not *then* seem jarring but natural: it was part and parcel of the divine and secular world view taken for granted in which logic, grammar, style, and belief were much more "integrated" than our own beliefs and our own much more complex institutions.

The connections all this has with the fairy stories is their inner logic and coherence. We must not forget that Perrault was trained as a lawyer, as May Hill Arbuthnot justly reminds us. It means that the stories were written with "outstanding logic without any loose ends unaccounted for, with every detail worked out to completion with legal precision . . . the kind of work one would expect from a legal mind."[13] The endings of some of the tales are good examples. In "Bluebeard" we are informed that the deceased husband had no heir, and thus his wife inherited his castle and his wealth. Perrault then explains that she used one share of the inheritance to enable her sister to get married to a nobleman who had been in love with her for many years, another share to purchase officers' commissions for her two brothers, and the last share, or "the remainder"—to use Perrault's expression—she used to get married, that is, we assume, to locate a husband in order to join her wealth with his, as was the custom of the bourgeoisie of those days. The endings of "Le Chat botté," "Cendrillon," and "Le Petit Poucet" also have the same legalistic precision. Such carefully thought endings point obviously to the mature mind of the sexagenarian father Perrault, rather than to that of the seventeen-year-old son Pierre as the author of the stories.

For Perrault, anything which is not necessary to the action or movement of the story should be cut out. He expressed this clearly in this striking statement: "one must compose as a painter and finish as a sculptor, that is to say, when one writes, first jot down many ideas on paper and then finish up by removing as much as possible. I sketch as a painter and I finish as a sculptor."[14] The best "show" of Perrault's mind at work is the comparison between the first and final state of "La Belle au bois dormant." This process of condensation or concision often results in a style full of understatements, ellipsis, and wit.

Such characteristics link his style with that of other classical authors of his age, particularly La Fontaine, Racine, and Pascal.

The resemblance with La Fontaine has often been noted. One could say that Perrault's three first tales in verse sound like works of La Fontaine. In *Les Souhaits ridicules* we find the suggestion that the "magical" misfortune of the peasant's wife, who could not talk very easily because she was afflicted with a long sausage welded to her nose, can be a boon to her husband who thought her too talkative anyway. All these ideas are expressed by us, but only inferred by Perrault.

> Cet ornement en cette place
> Ne faisait pas bon effet;
> Si ce n'est qu'en pendant sur le bas du visage
> Il l'empêchait de parler aisément,
> Pour un Epoux merveilleux avantage.[15]

> This decoration in such a spot
> Did not look very good;
> And in hanging in front of her mouth
> Prevented her from talking very easily,
> For a husband what a wonderful boon.

It is in the last two lines that we find a significant ellipsis, because the sentence would be more grammatically correct if it were stated thus: "prevented her from talking easily / Which for a husband is a wonderful boon."

This is the time, once again, to say: "Brevity is the soul of wit." Our explanation is already too long. In our translation of Perrault's key line, we should have left out the word "what" and the line should have read: "For a husband a wonderful boon." Poetry is a language in which affect is elicited by a mysterious relationship between context, meaning, and sound. And when it is felicitous, poetry, whether in verse or in prose, is characterized by its concinnity. That harmony between the parts, that melody of sound and meaning, that inner coherence of the work of art—such is the definition of concinnity. Not a word could be suppressed from the narratives we know as "Little Red Riding Hood," "Puss in Boots," "Cinderella," or "Hop O' My Thumb." Who could, who would dare change the perfect dialogue between the wolf and Red Riding Hood? Marcel Aymé, in his introduction to Perrault's *Contes*, is certainly right in writing

that he would shudder at the thought of what "Bluebeard" or
"Puss in Boots" might have become at the hands of either Boileau
or a twentieth-century "arranger" or "adaptator."

V *Perrault in English*

The stories of Perrault came into the English language, we
recall, with the 1729 translation of Robert Samber. There will
be no attempt here to repeat what has been said in other publications concerning that little known edition.[16] In the text
we will look for the ways in which the first translator dealt
with a material which was first very new, from across the Channel (or across the Atlantic), but then became very familiar.

The first English translation has something debonair and
attractive about it: the print is large and clear and the illustrations
of the original French edition are carefully reproduced; the text
is prefaced by an interesting letter of dedication to the countess
of Granville, which may well be the first criticism in English of
Perrault's tales. A crucial passage deserves to be quoted in its
entirety:

The Author of the following stories has happily succeeded . . . and
perhaps nothing yet extant can equal them in their admirable Design
and Execution. It was however observed that some of them were very
low and childish, especially the first, Little Red Riding Hood. It is
very true, and therein consists their Excellency. They therefore who
made this an Objection, did not seem very well to understand what
they said; they should have reflected that they are designed for Children; and yet the Author hath so ingeniously and masterly contrived
them, that they insensibly grow up, gradually one after another, in
Strength and Beauty, both as to their Narration and Moral, and are
told with such a Naiveté, and natural innocent Simplicity, that not only
Children, but those of Maturity, will also find in them uncommon
Pleasure and Delight.[17]

In this statement we encounter, for the first time, praise for the
"admirable Design and Execution" of the fairy tales. The way
in which Perrault had "contrived" them, however, does not correspond to Perrault's original order of publication. The first
story of the original manuscript and first edition was "Sleeping

Beauty," not "Little Red Riding Hood." The sequence followed is that of the French edition of 1721, and the practice was often adopted in subsequent reprints, probably in order to suggest a sort of gradation. "Little Red Riding Hood" must have seemed the most childish tale, followed by "The Fairies," "Bluebeard," "Sleeping Beauty," and "Puss in Boots"; afterward, the last three tales follow in the original order.

Samber ends his dedicatory letter with a witty criticism of English "Fabulists" who wrote for children at the time, the better to extoll, by implied contrast, the virtues of Perrault: "they content themselves in venting some poor insipid trifling Tale in a little tingling jingle, adding some pretty Witticisms, or insignificant useless Reflection, which they call a Moral, and think they have done the Business."[18] What he found in Perrault's text must have seemed to him the kind of narratives which adults and children of England had needed, as he wrote: "Strength and Beauty . . . uncommon Pleasure and Delight.[19]

As we read the English text we find amusing renditions of the original French. In "Little Red Riding Hood" the cakes of Perrault become custard pie, the woodcutters (*bûcherons*) become faggot-makers, and instead of using the expression "knock-knock at the door," Samber reproduces the French words used by Perrault: "Toc Toc." Whatever may have been his reasons for thus changing the text, the translator cannot be blamed for not using the word "woodcutter," which seems not only the most natural word to use, but also the most accurate translation: "woodcutter" probably did not then exist in the English language. Its first recorded use dates from 1774, in the *Pennsylvania Gazette*. In truth the word is an Americanism. In most English or American editions published since the beginning of the nineteenth century, the word "woodcutter" is used.

Other differences from the French text fall into three categories: they are either obvious mistakes in translation, examples of picturesque speech, or expressions of eighteenth-century English. Some mistakes are interesting. To translate the expression "elle ne se sentait pas de joie" (referring to Cinderella)—which means she was beside herself with joy—Samber wrote: "she appeared indifferent."[20] Most mistranslations are not worth signaling, but an extraordinary one occurs in "Bluebeard" and

refers to the terrifying moment when the unfortunate woman
discovers the bodies of the previous wives. The passage in
Samber's text reads: ". . . after some moments she began to
observe that the floor was all covered over with clotted blood,
on *which lay the bodies of several dead women ranged against
the walls*"[21] (our italics). Obviously the dead women could not
at the same time "lay" on the floor and be "ranged" against the
wall. This logical impossibility is the result of a careless translation. What the French text says is that the floor was covered
with clotted blood in which were reflected (*se miraient*) the
bodies of several women attached (or hanging) along the walls.
The bizarre translation quoted above was reproduced in the
first American edition (1794) and thus proves that the American
publisher simply reprinted Samber's translation.

Some samples of picturesque speech, even footnotes to the
translation by the translator, are significant. The wolf in "Little
Red Riding Hood," "compère le Loup," becomes "Gossop Wolf,"
which is more accurate—a term certainly closer to the French
meaning of the text than "Father Wolf," which we find in a
1912 English and American edition; it is certainly a more suggestive translation. In "Bluebeard" there is an oddly colloquial
and modern question: "How comes this blood upon the key?"[22]
In the same tale, we find it quaint that the wife and her sister
address each other with the archaic "thee" and "thou." The
famous question—"Anne, ma soeur Anne, ne vois-tu rien venir?"—
concerning the hoped-for arrival of the rescuing brothers, becomes: "Anne, sister Anne, dost thou see nothing coming?"[23]

In "Sleeping Beauty" and "Cinderella," the two tales which
contain so many realistic details, the translator was at a loss to
find expressions which would correspond to the original French
and therefore nicely anglicized his text. The enchanted palace
is guarded by Beefeaters and not by the traditional *Suisses*, the
mercenary soldiers used by French kings for their personal
protection. What we traditionally recognize as the famous "Hall
of Mirrors," or the "Galerie des Glaces," then not too familiar
in England, becomes the "Hall of looking glasses." There were
occasions when the translator had to give explanations concerning items probably not yet familiar to his English readers.
In 1729 this statement was added to the original text: "Now an

Ogre is a giant that has long teeth and claws, with a raw head and bloody bones, that runs away with naughty little boys and girls and eats them up."[24] Probably the most amusing extrapolation is a culinary note—the recipe for *Sauce Robert*—which the wicked mother-in-law orders for her dinner of Sleeping Beauty's daughter, Dawn (served as a royal stew): "*Sauce Robert* is a French sauce, made with minced onions, and boiled tender in butter, to which is added vinegar, mustard, salt, pepper, and a little wine."[25] A few translations stand out like commentaries on the text of Perrault and with one more quote—without by any means having exhausted the subject—we will end our treatment of the first appearance of Perrault in English. After Sleeping Beauty and her prince charming were married—a few hours after her awakening—they went to bed. The French text simply says that "they slept little, the princess had no great need of it."[26] The manifest meaning of the language used is clear: she did not sleep much, because she had slept already for one hundred years. The English translation, however, is more Gallic than the original, in that it suggests a latent or erotic meaning: "they slept very little; the Princess *had no occasion*"[27] (our italics).

If we have dwelt at length on this first translation, it is because we know that what we are discussing is largely unfamiliar to the majority of our readers; our main intent is to show that there was a beginning to the tradition of Sleeping Beauty and Cinderella in the English language: it started with a literary translation of Perrault. What happened afterward in England and in the United States is a story of constant change and adaptation, including bowdlerized versions—theater performances and film adaptations at all levels—adult or "childish." In this respect we should mention the Walt Disney film versions of "Cinderella" and "Sleeping Beauty," which have achieved world-wide diffusion without any acknowledgment of Perrault's authorship. In France the 1967 Jacques Demy film adaptation of *Peau d'Ane* with Jean Marais and Catherine Deneuve has been a great success.

Among the many translations which have appeared in this century, four stand out. The first is that of A. E. Johnson (1912), which has had a widespread "revival"[28] through the attractive reprint (1969) reproducing the large, beautiful, and suggestive illustrations of Gustave Doré, which first appeared in 1867. The second translation of note, partial though it is—only "Puss in Boots," "Sleeping Beauty" and "Cinderella"—is the work of the American poet Marianne Moore.[29] The quality of her translation is such that it lends plausibility even to her mistakes. She confuses the verb *plaire* ("to please") with the verb *pleurer* ("to weep"), with the interesting result that Sleeping Beauty and her prince "shed some tears" (after all, why not?), while all Perrault wrote was that the words of the prince-discoverer pleased (*plurent*) his paramour. This error is also present in the 1729 translation, and Marianne Moore may have made use of it. In general her text is imaginative and poetic: an "American" flavor pervades her versions. A magistrate becomes a "man with a great seal," and Puss wears his boots "like a general."

The translation of the English scholar of French literature, Geoffrey Brereton,[30] is certainly the most accurate. At least there are no mistakes due to his misunderstanding of the French language. The morals are also included; they were omitted in the Marianne Moore translation.

But the best and probably most *complete* translation of Perrault is that of Anne Carter,[31] who included the three verse tales. Her text is at least as careful as that of Geoffrey Brereton, and it is a pleasure to read Perrault's *Donkey-Skin* and *Griselda* in English. The illustrations are pleasant, but at times erroneous: Cinderella was not driven to the court ball in a carriage driven by *mice*.

The bibliography of translations of very popular works is not the kind of work frequently undertaken by literary scholars. However, for two stories of Perrault, "Puss in Boots" and "Cinderella," the bibliographical information can be found in the works of Denise Escarpit[32] and Anna Birgitta Rooth.[33] These books tell a tale of wide diffusion since the eighteenth century. Literature and popular traditions intermingle throughout the centuries.

VI *Perrault's Tales and Folklore and Literature*

One of the most common misconceptions about fairy tales is that the majority of them are folktales, merely collected from oral traditions and rarely the work of authors. It is true that many fairy tales are also folktales with a long oral history: there is quite a flowering of fairy tales in Russia where they, as well as folktales, are still told and read today. This is apparently also the situation in French Canada. There is a lively oral tradition in both countries.

The narratives of Perrault have been so enormously popular in the English language that they have become accepted as native English stories, perhaps replacing similar ones in oral tradition. We do not, however, have examples of Perrault's tales in either English or French popular tradition recorded *before* the publication of Perrault's *Contes de Ma Mère l'Oye*. We could—for a moment—accept the notion that he simply jotted tales down upon hearing some peasant woman telling the stories to his children. In that case we would agree with Iona and Peter Opie that: "If only it had occurred to him to state where he had obtained each tale, and when, and under what circumstances, he would today probably be revered as the father of folklore."[34] It is not Perrault who is revered as the father of folklore today but Jacob and Wilhelm Grimm who published their *Kinder und Hausmärchen* [Household Stories] in 1812–1815. They had bothered to state their "where and when and under what circumstances," even though they did not transcribe faithfully what they collected, but "improved" the style of folk informants.[35]

Perrault was, nevertheless, quite conscious of popular tradition. He referred to the success and wide distribution of chapbooks published in Troyes in the preface of his *Apologie des femmes*. In the *Correspondance* of the exiled Protestant writer Pierre Bayle, there is an interesting letter of the Abbé Jean-Baptiste Dubos concerning Perrault's research for *Griselidis*. He had read Boccaccio's version of the story (but apparently not that of Chaucer), and he also knew chapbook versions of *Griselidis*.[36] He mentions these as being printed on *papier bleu* ("blue paper"), the traditional color for chapbooks until the French Revolution. He was conscious of the tradition of the story before him, but we must not think of him in terms of a twentieth-century folklorist anxious to recapture the "soul" of the people. His chief source was Boccaccio, and not any specific folklore version. As was the custom of the time, he used the text of Boccaccio as a source of inspiration, and he wrote freely. One major difference of treatment in Perrault's text is that the daughter of Griselidis has a fiancé—a new character not found in Boccaccio.

For the other tales, notably the famous prose tales, Perrault has provided posterity with a long acknowledgment of his "popular" sources. The salient points of that statement were: the insistence of having "recorded naively [stories] the way he had heard them told in his childhood," the antiquity of the tales, and their moral value. Very few scholars have disputed that Perrault did not tell anything but the truth in these affirmations. It is possible, however, that such a statement reflects more a literary convention than it does the truth about the folk origin of the Mother Goose tales. Three hundred years ago nobody would readily admit authorship of children's stories such as fairy tales. They had to come, therefore, from some "infinite number of fathers, mothers, grandmothers, governesses and greatgrandfriends . . ." (Perrault's own words in the *Mercure Galant*, January 1697). Perrault, however, had also admitted having written these fairy tales in order to amuse his children.

The contradictory assumption—whether Perrault was the recorder of the tales or the writer of the tales—need not be defended: Perrault is both. There is no reason why he could not have used material from popular tradition—indeed, also from literary tradition before him—but he made all this material his own. Two examples from the realm of music will perhaps clarify this argument. Were not Chopin and Bartok inspired by Polish and Hungarian folksongs? And yet, all we know is their music, and there is a chance that the original folksongs they used as sources of inspiration may have become completely lost or forgotten. What we have is their music. And what we have are Perrault's stories.

Perrault's tales were so often reprinted and translated that they became very well-known not only in France but in the rest of Europe as well, and exerted a great influence on oral tradition. When the Grimm Brothers began gathering their German folktales for the publication of their famous collection, they found examples of all of the stories of Perrault in the German language. Some stories even had titles which were close translations from the French, such as "Rotkäppchen" [Red Riding Hood], "Blaubart" [Bluebeard], or "Aschenputtel" [Cinderella]. In the case of "Blaubart," the Brothers Grimm must have felt somewhat disturbed. The story, which was in fact printed in the first edition of 1812, disappears from all subsequent editions. That version of "Bluebeard" was in all respects similar to that of Perrault. According to Gilbert Rouger, "fearing that [it] could be nothing but a mere translation of Perrault's tale, they removed it"[37] and used another similar story of German origin, "Fitschers Vogel."

Thus, even in stories collected from German oral tradition, a story of Perrault's literary text reappears almost verbatim. There could be no clearer example of the influence, or diffusion, of a literary text into the stream of oral tradition. What happened was that the stories of Perrault were told *in French* and retold by French governesses entrusted with the education of German children during the eighteenth century, a period during which practically all Europe was affecting French manners and worshiping French culture and institutions. The diffusion of Perrault's tales in Germany has been well documented in the article of Harry Velten.[38] What is true of German tradition is even truer of English and American tradition, in which the stories of Perrault have achieved universal recognition while Perrault as their author is not very well known. Everyone has heard of "Sleeping Beauty" and "Cinderella," but who has heard of Perrault?

After the Brothers Grimm passed on, the science of folklore continued to flourish, culminating in the monumental *Motif-Index of Folk-literature*,[39] in which the very titles of Perrault's tales were found to be so universal that they reappear as subtitles in the basic folklore nomenclature. The oral stories collected by folklorists in this and the last century still reflect the influence of Perrault. Specialists of folklore have fully acknowledged the importance of Perrault in this respect: "Largely because of the influence of Perrault's collection of fairy tales, one of the best known of all stories of helpful animals is "Puss in Boots".... Perrault's French version . . . has been of primary influence on the traditions of this tale."[40] Another authority on folklore goes even further: "Perrault's version . . . has been taken as *the* version almost everywhere and has altered the detail of the older folk form everywhere that it has penetrated."[41]

The simple truth about Perrault is not that he was a collector of folklore material: he was a great inventor and artist, certainly inspired by popular tradition, but above all one of the greatest influences on the folklore of the western world. His contribution has resulted in the crystallization of a few images and types that have for some reason stuck in our "collective" imagination. The mention of Cinderella immediately elicits a few images: the persecuted stepchild, the kitchen maid, the fairy godmother, the ball, the pumpkin carriage, the glass slipper. Of all these images, the carriage, the slipper, and the idea of midnight "curfew" are probably the best known. We all too easily forget that the simplest, clearest, and most effective version was that of Perrault, and that it appeared over a hundred years before the version of the Brothers Grimm. Both versions have become immensely popular, at least in the United States, through numerous editions (accurate and "vulgarized"), including the famous film version of Walt Disney: the tale has become ubiquitous, truly part of the oral tradition of our century. Everyone knows, or thinks he knows, the story of Cinderella. But usually one confuses unknowingly Perrault and Grimm. Thus the carriage of Perrault's version is frequently remembered (as well as the pumpkin from which it was made), but it does not appear at all in the Grimms' text. But who really cares? It is characteristic of commonly accepted images that very few of those who use them know their origins. If an American adolescent says "after midnight I turn into a pumpkin," does she realize that she is inaccurately echoing Perrault's text?

To clarify the connection between Perrault and folklore, we will list below a few reference works (cited also in the bibliography). There is, first of all, Stith Thompson's *The Folktale* (1946), which suggests that much research needs to be done on the "stylistic interaction between the literary and the oral folktale,"[42] while admitting the enormous influence of Perrault.

In France itself the central work is the comprehensive two-volume *Catalogue du Conte merveilleux français* [Catalogue of the French Wonder Tale, 1957–1964] by the late Paul Delarue and Marie-Louise Tenèze, in which we find Perrault's tales classified according to the international nomenclature of Aarne-Thompson's *Motif-Index*, as well as some interesting remarks on the influence of Perrault. Paul Delarue was a folklorist first and foremost. He believed that the oral "pure" folktale was superior to the literary fairy tale. Consequently, anything in Perrault which seems too refined and too widely imitated by other authors, he does not consider the authentic voice of the people. Delarue could not fully admire Perrault, and lamented his influence on the score of women fairy tale authors who published in the last ten years of the seventeenth century. He decried as well the enormous flowering of the fairy tale in the eighteenth century, resulting in the forty-one volumes of the *Cabinet des Fées*,[43] published just before the French Revolution (1785–1789). But these authors and their collections belong to literature and not to folklore—even though it is sometimes difficult to distinguish one from the other.

We have ample evidence of the diffusion of Perrault in the "popular" stream through numerous reprints in chapbooks during the eighteenth and nineteenth centuries. In our century, the French scholars Pierre Brochon, Geneviève Bollème,[44] and Robert Mandrou[45] have published well-documented volumes which attest once again to the influence of Perrault and the ubiquity of the fairy tale in all chapbook collections.

VII   *The Moral and Psychological Import of Perrault*

In previous pages we have mentioned the morals of Perrault's tales. The simple truth is that the moral message of the Mother Goose stories is rather pedestrian, utilitarian, and at times rather cynical. We see no profound ethical lesson in what happens in "Puss in Boots," "Bluebeard," or "Hop O' My Thumb." We do not find much inspiration either in the versified morals of these stories.

Yet Perrault, like La Fontaine, professed to be moral and offered his stories as educational tales for the betterment of the young. It is possible that both La Fontaine and Perrault believed that their fables and tales possessed an educational value. It is also possible that in their days a lesson of opportunism might pass for a moral lesson. We profess a much broader ethical conception. For us there is ethical value in any narrative that becomes a classic. Such a narrative gives an impression of order and beauty, rhythm and elegance. Children, and *a fortiori* adults, become better human beings through the experience of beautiful narratives. Paul Hazard stated in *Books, Children and Men*, one of the most suggestive books ever written about children's litera-

ture, that nursery rhymes do not seem "unconscious of the fact
that by placing rhythm at the beginning of life they are conform-
ing to the general order of the universe."[46] The statement applies
to the tales of Perrault, if we paraphrase it thus: fairy tales, by
their recital of immemorial adventures told at the beginning of
youth, tell the child that he belongs to the same universal order
as that of heroes and heroines in the supernatural world.

The child perceives that fairy tales are symbolic narratives
even if he does not understand them fully. For a child, "Little
Red Riding Hood" is a story about the danger of wolves, a warning tale that has been well analyzed in semiological terms.[47] But
for an adult the story can be ironic because he reads the narrative
as an allegory of sexual seduction. The "obscure" way in which
the child may still have an awareness of the symbolic import of
any kind of narrative is of enormous educational importance.
For, if the child accepts a fairy tale at face value, there must be
something wrong with his emotional makeup. It is through the
fairy tale that he may first learn the difference between fiction
and reality. He learns to accept fairy tales as beautiful fictions
which enrich his innermost mind. Perrault understood this very
well when he wrote that fairy tales are like "seeds that one
throws, which first bring forth the emotions of joy and sadness,
but which will inevitably bloom later in the form of worthy
feelings."[48]

Furthermore, since fairy tales are first told or read aloud to
children by parents or friends, they act as an emotional bridge
between adult and young. Each enjoys the tale in his own way:
the adult pretending to become young again and a believer of
fairies, the child dreaming of supernatural powers like those of
the wonder-tale heroes. But that emotional bridge is also an
aesthetic bridge. When both an adult and a child pretend to
believe in a fairy tale, not because it is absolutely convincing,
but because it is beautifully expressed, they become "aesthetic
accomplices?

In that large ethical and aesthetic sense, Perrault's fairy
tales acquire a new dimension. They have been told and retold
so often that they seem immortal: Sleeping Beauty, Puss in Boots,
Cinderella are reborn with each new generation of children. Such
characters have become legendary in our Western culture (and

probably outside of it, in China or Japan as well). We fully agree with the statement of Mircea Eliade that the fairy tale has an initiatory function in our civilization: "Without realizing it, and thinking he is merely entertaining himself or escaping, modern man still enjoys the imaginary initiation which fairy tales bring to him."[49]

Eliade is here comparing the fairy tale to the legends and myths told the young in "primitive" societies. In the context of these cultures it is through the recital of the deeds of heroic ancestors that the young learn of their forefathers—whom they are urged to imitate. It might be argued that insofar as the fairy tales are concerned they do not contain any adventures or feats as heroic as those that can be found in such epics as the *Iliad* or the *Odyssey*. We do not agree. The characters of Perrault, because of their interesting combination of stylization and psychological appeal, are the kind of heroes whom the young—consciously or unconsciously—want to imitate. A young girl readily daydreams about the fate of Cinderella, a young boy might easily dream of owning such a wonderful "gadget" as the seven-league boots.

In those dreams reside the fulfillment of life, as Joseph Campbell beautifully expressed it: "... they are the heroes and villains who have built the world for us. The debutante combing her hair before the glass, the mother pondering the future of a son, the laborer in the mines, the merchant vessel full of cargo, the ambassador with portfolio, the soldier in the field of war—all are working in order that the ungainsayable specifications of effective fantasy, the permanent patterns of the tale of wonder, shall be clothed in flesh and known as life."[50] In another passage, Campbell emphasizes the symbolic content of fairy tales: "The function of the craft of the tale ... was not simply to fill the vacant hour, but to fill it with symbolic fare. And since symbolization is the characteristic pleasure of the human mind, the fascination of the tale increased in proportion to the richness of its symbolic content."[51]

The psychological import of Perrault's tales derives from their symbolic content. Each symbol has its corresponding psychological resonance. The recent book of Bruno Bettelheim provides explanations or rather a psychoanalysis of about fifteen fairy tales, most from the Grimms' collection, a few from Perrault's. Since his work has achieved a great popularity—and been translated into French—no analytical discussion of Perrault's fairy tales is now possible without referring to it. In many ways Bettelheim seems to have interpreted Perrault's stories in a thoroughly definitive way, as only a psychoanalyist and a child psychiatrist could. We will give an account of his interpretations. But we do not wish to suggest that we entirely agree with him.

To discern a symbol is to explain how we think, or vibrate inwardly with its message. In "Sleeping Beauty," Perrault articulated the idea of sleep as a symbol for the passive, introspective period of puberty: "This is how the symbolic language of the fairy tale states that after having gathered strength in solitude the young have now become themselves."[52] Perrault emphasized the value of "sleep" as a period of learning when he told his audience not to be amazed if the princess was perfectly alert, pert, and articulate after her century of sleep: "she had plenty of time to think and learn through the many pleasant dreams her fairy had inspired in her."[53] This remark of Perrault—which some may dislike or dismiss as an extraneous interpolation—is peculiar to his version.

"Bluebeard" is a story of sexual transgression. In her husband's absence the wife has been unfaithful. It is a terrifying story suggesting that on a "preconscious level the child understands from the indelible blood on the key and from other details that Bluebeard's wife has committed a sexual indiscretion."[54] But he was wrong in seeking such a cruel revenge (death by beheading). The tale teaches deep down a higher morality, which Bettelheim finds expressed by Perrault himself in the second moral: "One can well see that this is a story of times past; / There are no longer such terrible husbands who demand the impossible / Even when they are dissatisfied or jealous, / They act gently toward their wives."[55]

We have no difficulty in accepting Perrault's point of view as expressed above. But the explanation of Bettelheim that the key and the forbidden room symbolize sexual infidelity can be open to question. There is no doubt that the two motifs do suggest sex—as many dreams and stories have confirmed—but there is not the slightest reference within the story as told by Perrault that another man was present in any form in the life or the thoughts of Bluebeard's wife. Fairy tales are usually very explicit narratives, even though they may be highly symbolic. What disturbs us in Bettelheim's explanations is that he does not seem to grant the possibility that any story or element of a story can be interpreted in more ways than one (his own). Perhaps the story as told by Perrault is also valid as an allegory of infant curiosity and adult cruelty, including the possibility of sexual curiosity, but not excluding either Perrault's plainly manifest content and interpretation.

The tale which has been the most elaborately interpreted by Bettelheim is "Cinderella." We will not repeat all he wrote concerning the interpretation of Cinderella's slipper as a symbol for the vagina. We are, in fact, quite ready to agree with him. A ring or a slipper are common motifs in fairy tales, and easy to interpret as such. We disagree with him concerning the character of Perrault's heroine. He feels that she is passively "sugar sweet and insipidly good . . . and completely lacks initiative."[56] No, the Cinderella of Perrault is, on the contrary, very alive, very spirited, and full of initiative. Any reader of this tale (in French or in an English translation) can see for himself: all he has to do is read the dialogues between Cinderella and her fairy godmother, or her conversations with her sisters, or the account of the ball at the royal palace, or the reference to the laughter of Cinderella pulling out of her pocket the other slipper which she had kept all along.

Another instance where we feel Bettelheim has failed to understand something essential—in fact, thoroughly missing a plausible interpretation—is the case of the famous carriage. The idea of the carriage itself he finds a useless addition to the story, as we have already shown. He explains at great length how the fairy scoops the pumpkin and transforms it into a beautiful carriage; then, following the opinion of Marc Soriano, he considers that in this episode Perrault treats the magical in an ironic way (he may well be right) which detracts from the beauty and wonder of the story (an opinion which can be debated).

Applying Bettelheim's own method of interpretation and analysis, we suggest the following. The carriage is *essential* for Cinderella. Dressed as she was in regal clothes, she could not—

in her own social context of 1697—go to the ball on foot. Furthermore, she needed its *protection* and *comfort*. The thoughtful fairy wanted her ward to have some kind of parental protection, be it in the form of a carriage, to go "out in the world alone." We recall the act of scooping the inside of the pumpkin, transforming it into the golden carriage, and finally placing Cinderella inside of it and sending her along. This sequence begs for interpretation. Cinderella was a stepchild without a mother. What the fairy did was to create symbolically a womb (the pumpkin) in which she placed Cinderella, who was reborn again inside of it, as a full blown woman ready to mate, ready to meet her prince. This obvious analysis seems to have escaped our analyst.

There is one other point about this tale we wish to make. Bettelheim insists that Perrault is too interested in clothes as an outward symbol of wealth, and that he does not pay enough attention to the *character* of Cinderella, where clothes are unimportant. We beg to differ. Here is a reference to the beauty "without clothes" of Cinderella: "Cinderella, notwithstanding her raggedy clothes, was a hundred times more beautiful than her sisters who were so luxuriously dressed."[57] As to the fact that the prince or his entourage ought to have been able to recognize Cinderella after the ball when she was dressed in her usual ugly clothes (as is the fact in the Grimm version), we will simply recall that when the nobleman in charge of trying the slipper comes face to face with Cinderella, he disregards the sarcasms of the wicked sisters, and "having looked intently at Cinderella, and having found her quite beautiful,"[58] proceeds with the famous slipper test.

We do not wish to "overargue" our case concerning Cinderella, but it so happens that, in preparing the Perrault *Concordance,* we have *copied* with our own hands the text of Perrault, and know almost by heart all the fairy tales. We have practically total recall of the text of our author.

In general the book of Bruno Bettelheim gives the impression of a "grammar of symbols," a sort of closed world in which symbols are explained once and for all. We feel that context is of the essence in the explanation of symbols. True, they may be a universal language, but only in a kind of dynamic dialectic sense, in the exchange that takes place between the story (or producer of the story) and its listeners or readers. It is all a question of psychic resonance within a given sociocultural context.

We will only briefly deal with "Puss in Boots." We agree that it is an amoral story. The hero's success is arranged through shameless deceit and effrontery. The same can be said about "Tom Thumb." In both these tales the youngest child, the most underprivileged, finally prevails, thanks to his resourcefulness. The function of such tales is not to give a choice between good and bad, but to give a child hope that even someone as small and as disinherited as he may be, can, like the peasant boy of "Puss in Boots," "Tom Thumb," or "Jack the Giant Killer," succeed in life.[59] There is also in "Puss in Boots" a totemic element: the animal is here the protector-provider of his master, just as in American Indian tribal legend a certain animal is the totem or protector of the clan.

"Beauty and the Beast" is the last story which Bettelheim interprets. Perrault's variation of that theme is "Riquet à la houppe." Everything that Bettelheim writes on the subject seems quite relevant and correct. The beast as a sexual symbol is quite obvious, quite easy to discern from the various narratives he analyzes. "Riquet à la houppe" is not treated at length; it is the object of a long footnote.[60] The story of Perrault can only be understood as a version of "Beauty and the Beast," within a tradition of tales originating with the myth of Cupid and· Psyche. We presented (in 1960 and in 1975)—prior to Bettelheim—our analyses of both the myth and the fairy tale,[61] and Bettelheim's interpretation coincides with our own.

Furthermore, on the question of "Riquet à la houppe," we feel that a fuller analysis is necessary. There are two stories by that name, that of Mlle Bernard, which appeared before Perrault's in 1696, and that of our author, published the following year. The main difference between the two stories consists in the fact that in Mlle Bernard's version Riquet marries his princess before the end of the tale; she tires of him and manages to have an affair with a friend she hides in the palace. Riquet punishes his wife in an unusual way: he transforms the handsome lover into his twin brother, with the result that the princess is condemned to live with two husbands, not knowing which of the two she should hate.

Perrault's version is much simpler. As we know, the princess has no lover. We recall that when she agreed to marry Riquet, he seemed immediately to be transformed into a handsome man. The clever explanation that it was love that made the princess find the ugly Riquet suddenly handsome is Perrault's refined way of suggesting discreetly that his story is a symbolic account of the power of sexual attraction. It is also clear that Perrault knew the previous version of his story, and saw fit to eliminate the lover. In his story the lover and the husband coincide. The moment Riquet is accepted as a sexual person he becomes attractive. But this acceptance of Riquet as a sexual companion is an expression of maturity: his wife welcomes him as he really is, and as adult wisdom demands according to psychological truth and custom.

In conclusion we must say that not all of Perrault's stories have been completely interpreted to our satisfaction. On the story of *Donkey-Skin*, with its obvious incestuous element of a father seeking to marry his daughter, we have not found any analytical criticism. We are also surprised that the Grimm Brothers' version of that tale (*Allerleirauh*, or Skin of all Animals), in which the father finally *marries* his daughter, is not even mentioned.[62]

A major work of synthesis remains to be written on the interpretation of all fairy tales, not only those of Perrault. This work would show that after myths, which are the easiest to interpret, the fairy tales offer the simplest structures and styles. Like dreams, myths and fairy tales are the royal road to the unconscious. Among authors of fairy tales Perrault seems to us one of the best, because of a style which is at once simple, or naive, and yet very refined in its gentle humor and irony. That combination of refinement and naiveté is not unique to Perrault. It is present in all the great authors of fairy tales: Mme. d'Aulnoy, Mme Léprince de Beaumont, Andersen and Lewis Carroll, to name but a few. Their literary charm enhances our world and constantly elicits interpretations wherein we find images of our complex psychic selves.[63]

CHAPTER 6

Last Years and Last Works

I War and Peace During the Declining Years of the Sun King

THE last twenty-three years of Perrault's life span the period
1680–1703. We have already accounted for his most important productions during those years: the four volumes of the
Parallèle, the *Hommes illustres*, the *Apologie des femmes*, and,
of course, the fairy tales. However, during the period he published these works he was also producing an additional, fairly
large body of prose and poetry.

We have a somewhat different perspective than Perrault's concerning the wars Louis XIV waged during the last years of the
seventeenth century. The first set of wars of the French king,
during the 1670s, had involved his army and navy in a contest
of strength against the Netherlands and their German allies. The
net result had been a stalemate between France and the rest
of Europe, as expressed in the Treaty of Nimwegen (1679). The
peace that ensued was uneasy. For the Dutch, the Spaniards, the
Germans, and (secretly) the English had come to detest the
name of France and that of Louis XIV. The ruthlessness of
French soldiery, in both peace and war, in the occupied terri-
tories (especially in Holland and in the German Palatinate) had
not endeared the king of France abroad. Even contemporary
French historians are generally agreed in condemning the wars
of the Sun King as counterproductive and often cruel. Louis's
overblown ego seems to have been the cause of many of his
wars. His diplomacy was often too aggressive. He would annex
towns on his German borders if they had ever, in past centuries,
paid tribute to French princes. He called it the "right of reunion."

Charles Perrault in 1682, the year he retired from public
service, was probably not aware of the negative feelings har-

127

bored against his king in foreign courts. He could not quite understand that in Berlin there were Prussian princes who could not forgive Louis XIV for having forced them to restore Western Pomeramia to Sweden; nor could he understand how fiercefully anti-French the Hapsburgs had become because they had been humiliated in having to recognize the superiority of the Bourbon king. But the most implacable enemy of France was the Dutch prince William of Orange, who was soon to acquire an outstanding English general who heretofore had been serving Louis XIV. The name of that general, John Churchill, duke of Marlborough, is an illustrious one. The circumstances in which he "defected" are interesting. In the spring of 1685 Churchill had come to Versailles as unofficial ambassador of his king, James II of England (in fact he came to give thanks for the unsolicited French gift of five hundred thousand pounds). During his Versailles stay Churchill had stated that "if the king yielded to certain influences causing him to alter religion, he, Churchill, would no longer serve him."[1] In other words, Churchill was warning Louis XIV not to persecute Protestants.

That warning was not heeded. The French king was over-confident. Since Europe was then at peace, and James II was openly Catholic, he thought he could launch his grand project of proclaiming France entirely Catholic through the Revocation of the Edict of Nantes. In France itself—at least among Catholics—the measure was popular. The French king appeared to his subjects as a zealous reformer, and it seemed right to have a country with one king and one religion. In reality, far from creating a religiously united country the anti-Protestant measures brought disorder, rebellions, and an insidious kind of civil war. The persecutions were violent, and Protestants fled in droves to Germany, Switzerland, Holland, and England. With the hindsight of history we see that the Revocation of 1685 was a colossal mistake. Louis XIV had now made enemies of all countries where French Protestants had fled. Eventually the Catholic James II of England was dethroned by his father-in-law, William of Orange, and the Dutch ruler became king of England as well. But worse was to come—after a series of French victories across the Rhine. In the fall of 1688 Louis XIV made the pivotal mistake of his military career: he decided to invade Germany.[2]

At first all went well. During the months of September and October French armies swept through the German countryside, taking half a dozen cities in their wake. The king's son, the grand Dauphin, accompanied the triumphant armies and was present at the siege and capture of the fortress of Philippsburg.

The Rhineland and the Palatinate were in French hands during most of the winter of 1688–1689. A year later, William of Orange, now William III of England, was consolidating his armies and navies under the direction of John Churchill. Holland and England were now effectively united against France. In the heart of winter French troops began a strategic retreat from their German conquest, devastating the Palatinate on their way back to France. Atrocities upon atrocities were perpetrated—probably without the French king clearly understanding what was happening.

And now from all Germany, the Netherlands, and England there rose a great clamor for vengeance. The historian John Wolf is right in stating that the European coalition's struggle against France (1688–1698) was effectively the "First World War."[3] For Perrault, then a man in his early sixties, there was only one side of the story: his king could only be right both in his religious policies and in his wars. It was France surrounded by enemies, and the heroes were all on the French side. He could not realize that unprovoked French aggressions for territorial expansion were doomed to fail.

The foregoing historical sketch—however summary—is necessary for an understanding of much that Perrault wrote during these years of complex wars and political unrest. What he wrote falls mainly into three headings: works of "official" praise in which he continues as panegyrist of his king and century; a few works of religious inspiration; works of more purely personal inspiration, in which Perrault forgets either his king or his God and simply tells what he feels on various subjects without any polemic intent.

II *Public Writer and Poet Again*

Perrault had begun his career as an occasional or public poet. Now that he had retired from his employ as civil servant, one of his first efforts was again a poem concerning the royal family.

This time the occasion was the birth of the first royal grandchild. The grand Dauphin's wife had just been delivered of a child, and Perrault joined the chorus of public acclaim. The year is 1682, the title of the work is *Banquet des dieux pour la naissance du duc de Bourgogne* [Banquet of the Gods for the birth of the duke of Burgundy]. The work is complex, a mélange of prose and poetry in which Perrault introduces an interesting mythological fiction. He imagines that he himself goes up in the cloudy realm of Polymnia (or Polyhymnia), the muse of sacred or lyrical poetry and music. The muse invites the poet to hide with her in a cloud and be an invisible witness to the festivities which Jupiter (Louis XIV) is ordering in honor of the new birth. We are now in a supernatural realm, a sort of heavenly highway full of "gods and goddesses of all sorts and all ranks, most in fantastic carriages . . . shells pulled by fishes, others on little chariots pulled by sparrows and bats."[4] Mary Elisabeth Storer is right in stating that such carriages are close prefigurations of the pumpkin carriage in Cinderella.[5] This *Banquet* is a heady work in which verse passages seem to be sung in a fantastic operalike setting. A rather amusing passage is that of Silenus—the god of wine—toasting the king of France: "[may] his thunder producing sword / Deliver the whole earth / Of that despicable race of men who do not drink wine."[6] The reference must have been a veiled allusion to those beer drinkers, the German people on the other side of the Rhine.

The verve, the wit, and the felicitous combination of prose and poetry contribute to give the impression that this is another unjustly neglected work of Perrault that should be reprinted. In a final passage the author informs us that this work was set to music by Oudot and was in fact performed as an opera, or rather as an *opera buffa* at Versailles for the entertainment of the Dauphine princess.[7] It is regrettable that Perrault did not continue in this light vein. He had found a way to praise without appearing to praise.

The works we are now going to discuss are mostly poems of official praise which certainly lengthen the list of his productions without necessarily making his fame greater.

In 1687 Perrault had celebrated the recovery of Louis XIV from dangerous surgery for an anal fistula. That was the occasion for a rather well-known poem, *Le Siècle de Louis le Grand,* which we have already discussed. Another poem celebrated that event, entitled "Epistre au roi . . . sur l'excès de joie que Paris témoigna de la convalescence de Sa Majesté" [Epistle to the King . . . on the extreme joy which the People of Paris felt concerning the convalescence of His Majesty]. The most interesting part of the poem is precisely what we have just quoted: the very title. It conveys the idea that there were spontaneous manifestations of public joy at the time in the streets of Paris. Perrault must have been the witness of such popular expressions. His poem might have made excellent reading if he had been inspired to develop what his title seemed to promise. But he chose, instead, to revert to his pet idea of the superiority of his time, and simply "rehashed" what he had just written in his *Siècle de Louis le Grand.*

The following year (1688) he was better inspired by a military event, the siege and fall of the German strategic fortress of Philippsburg. This fortress was the easternmost point of French penetration during the campaign of 1688. The Dauphin was nominally in command of the French troops as they stormed the German stronghold. According to the historian Wolf the part played by Louis XIV's son in the siege of Philippsburg "was not significant."[8] Nevertheless, the proud king was overjoyed that his son had been present at that French victory. Perrault's poem, "A Monseigneur Le Dauphin sur la prise de Philippsbourg" [Ode To My Lord the Dauphin on the taking of Philippsburg], is a harmonic resonance of his king's joy. It bears little closeness to what really must have happened. Nevertheless, the not too lengthy series of eighty octosyllabic lines reads pleasantly. It is pure military, patriotic poetry, which must be read with a sense of its historical context. At the end of the poem Perrault rhetorically assumes that the captured citizens of Philippsburg address the Dauphin:

> But Philippsburg filled with fear
> Summons you to submit to your laws,
> Opens its bosom to you, and surrenders arms,
> Terrorized at the name of France.
> 'Tis a Terror whose vast Powers
> Were born under LOUIS'

Fame of glorious deeds;
'Tis a terror without restraint,
Without limits, and having become so
Great that the whole world is filled with it.[9]

We are not implicitly or explicitly approving or praising the
feelings expressed by Perrault in this poem; we are simply suggesting that as "official and patriotic" poetry these lines of our
author ring authentic.

Two years later, on October 3, 1690, Perrault was enjoying a
vacation in the village of Rosières, near Troyes, in the province
of Champagne, and was inspired to write his "Ode à Messieurs
de l'Académie française" [Ode to the French Academy]. It is
one of his best poems, consisting of nine stanzas of twenty octosyllabic lines, extolling the pleasure of living in the quiet countryside and praising the king and his armies for their heroic defense of France, again attacked by a European coalition. French
lyrical poetry does not translate well and has a way of sounding
trite in English. Here are a few lines of description of the country:

In the beautiful clime where the Seine river
Is nothing but a small stream
Meandering among pleasant meadows,
Graced by its flowing waters,
Fortunate fields are every year
Engoldened at harvest time
In generous abundance,
And hills warmed to high heat
Yield to those living in cabins
The most exquisite beverages
For quenching their thirst.

Our translation is not too literal, but we hope it conveys something of the charm of the original. In another stanza Perrault
tries to depict the wheat fields ready to harvest:

Here the furrows are greening again,
Giving forth the life hidden in seeds.
Further afield I see the earth opened
And traced by black lines where
The plow had trod.

Everywhere I see barns filled
With the rich harvested hay
Yielded by the plains,
Fragrant with that heady perfume
Which in the coolness
Of a beautiful evening,
Rises from the golden harvest
Of fields blessed by the Lord.

After such elegiac evocations the poem comes back to "reality" and tells Perrault's colleagues about the king at war against the rest of Europe. The last lines of the poem, in their anti-English feeling, are interesting:

Against that Tyrant
Who now ruthlessly rules England,
Who inspires horror in heaven and earth,
I will not utter any curses.
Divine justice is irritated enough
And urges to destroy him.
Your arm, Justice, will destroy and subdue him,
Ready to strike, like thunder
Howling and hovering over his head,
Awaiting the right moment.[10]

The "tyrant" mentioned by Perrault is William of Orange, at that time just victorious over James II of England (in spite of Louis XIV's help). Perrault's verbal attacks against William did not prevent him from becoming king of England and joining a colossal grand alliance of England, Spain, the Austrian Empire, Denmark, Savoy, and of course Holland. In engagements that foreshadowed the Napoleonic Wars the French king managed to muster a huge army of 450,000 soldiers.

Perrault tried to understand what was happening in the battlefields, and to respond with his pen. But these were difficult days. Louvois, the ruthlessly efficient minister of war who had mobilized such enormous resources in men and material, suddenly died. The monarch now took charge as commander in chief. The wars of the last years of the century were becoming quite murderous: as many as twenty thousand casualties suffered by the

European coalition and eight thousand on the French side at
the battle of Neerwinden near Brussels in 1693. Perrault was
probably not aware of the extent of this slaughter. All that he
mentioned in his poetry were the cities conquered; as, for instance, in the "Ode au roi" [Ode to the King, 1693]. The tone
of this poem is too conventionally cold and academically pom-
pous: too much thunder, too much glory, and too many instant
victories of a godlike king. The last stanzas of the ode depict
with some details the "infamous defeat / Of the proud Tyrant
of the English,"[11] and Perrault finally alludes to the plight of
war and the longing of the nation for peace, referring to Louis
XIV as a king with the heart of a father when he sees his subjects suffer. The year 1694 was a gloomy one even away from
the battlefield; there were dismal crops, widespread famine, and
everywhere enormous inflation caused by war expenses, nearly
three times above the treasury generated income.

There was a shortage of money—if not also of soldiers—on both
sides of the armed conflict, and popular resentment about continuous heavy taxations to finance such gigantic wars. In a speech
at the French Academy, "Réponse à Monsieur l'Abbé de Caumartin" [Answer to the Abbé de Caumartin, 1694], Perrault gives
in prose more felicitous than most of his verses a sort of portrait
of the French king, praising him in particular for his eloquence:
"Granted that our prince has a near magical power of statement,
let us not forget that he never abuses his facility for speaking;
he never uses words in anger or in scorn (because he knows too
well the force and influence of his words) . . . soon [Perrault
concludes] we shall see peace together with prosperity, crown
the heroic works of our monarch, and lavish upon us all the
bounties of the world."[12]

Peace did come, and Perrault continued to eulogize his king
for it[13] through the last months of his life. In 1701 he gave a
short speech at the Academy: "Réponse au Discours de Reception
de M. de Sacy" [Answer to the Admission Speech of M. de
Sacy]. The *Réponse* mentions one of the most important events
of Louis XIV's reign, the accession of his grandson (Philippe V)
to the throne of Spain, a triumph of diplomacy rather than of
war, for a change, at the request of the late king Charles II, and
the popular will as well: "this nation so proud and bellicose, on

their own free will, and without coercion, demands a master designated by our king."[14] In the same year Perrault wrote an "Ode au roi Philippe V allant en Espagne" [Ode to King Philip V going to Spain], an indifferent poem. In vain does one look for a powerful image, an ingenious metaphor to relieve the tedium of conventional praise.

The last poem of public praise of our author is dedicated not to the king of France but to that of Sweden. A short chapter could be written about Perrault and that northern country. He did not, like Descartes, travel there, but was associated with the diplomat Daniel Cronström and the architect Nicodemus Tessin during their stay in Paris. In 1693, Cronström came to Perrault to ask his advice on art and architecture which he relayed to his correspondents in Stockholm. It was the beginning of a warm friendship. Perrault provided his Swedish friend with information about Versailles and other royal residences. He also arranged for Louis XIV to entertain Cronström and allow him to show engravings of public buildings in Sweden. At that time Copenhagen was part of Sweden, and a royal castle was being built there, for which French and Italian models were examined. All this greatly interested Perrault. In many ways he was a professor of fine arts to his Swedish friends. In numerous letters to the Stockholm based Tessin, Cronström tells about Perrault "grabbing plans . . . promising a dissertation" and generally showing much enthusiasm concerning both the past (what had been built in France) and the present, what was being built in Sweden. Many drawings and plans which Perrault gave Cronström can now be seen in the National Library in Stockholm.

We are dwelling a bit on this episode to show that Perrault was not entirely chauvinistic in his outlook and could turn outside of France in his artistic interests. One could also contend that he may have been, in part, motivated by interest. The Cronström-Tessin correspondence mentions Perrault's offer to sell his Swedish friend quite a few art objects, notably a small organ, "for he is not doing very well these days."[15]

Since Perrault had such close Swedish friends they must have informed him at length about their country and their king. In the last years of the century Charles XII of Sweden was an outstanding military figure whom Perrault must have admired: king

of his country at fifteen, and at eighteen, victorious over the Russian troops of Czar Peter the Great at the battle of Narva
(November 20, 1700) in which eight thousand Swedes defeated
forty thousand Russians. We recall that in March of that same
year Perrault's son Pierre, a lieutenant in the elite Dauphin Regiment, had died. We suggest that Charles Perrault, having lost
a soldier son aged twenty-two, may well have felt some sort of
affinity for the northern king of eighteen who led his troops to
victory with such bravery. His "Ode pour le Roi de Suède"
[Ode to the King of Sweden, 1701] is different from his other
occasional poems. It is shorter than most, consisting of thirty-six
lines only. It is a well-informed poem, in which Perrault does not
praise excessively. Addressing the "trembling leaders" who opposed Charles XII, Perrault reminds them that large numbers of
soldiers do not necessarily ensure victory: "See how little success
so much courage in combat / Has caused so much death in your
ranks, filling whole fields with bodies; / And see if it is true
that Heaven favors / The side with the most battalions."

At the end of the poem Perrault alludes to the physical charm
of the young king who was loved by so many women. His bravery
is also praised: in trying to protect one of his generals Charles
XII deliberately put himself under enemy fire. His general,
nevertheless, was killed. Since this poem may be the last one
Perrault wrote let us quote the final stanza, unusual for the ideas
expressed:

> There are no great feats that could surprise anyone
> When glory adopts a twenty-year-old Hero
> Who still at a tender age
> Has triumphed without pain or toil
> Over pernicious indolence and vice.[16]

The feeling is new and vigorously expressed. Could it be that
this praise of self-control and stoicism is a pious wish referring
to the lost son? Could the lost son have been the antithesis of the
courageous twenty-year-old king?

III   The Religious Vein

Works of religious inspiration do not appear in Perrault's youth
but during the years of his retirement, after 1682. His first work

in this vein, "Épitre chrétienne sur la pénitence" [Christian Epistle on Penance, 1684], may be one of his best. It could more accurately be titled "Epistle on Suffering," for that is its real subject. The poem, written in the formal format of the classical Alexandrine couplet in which all the tragedies of Corneille and Racine were written, is one hundred and seventy-eight verses long. Knowing what we know of Perrault's life, we cannot help thinking that there are echoes of or veiled personal allusions to his own life. Even though the poem is addressed to a friend called Cléon, it could well be that the poet is speaking to himself when he recalls the cruel double loss of a son and of a wife: "Death, refusing to hear your prayers / . . . for ever took away your beloved son, / And then with an even more cruel hand / Came to tear away your faithful companion."[17]

There are lyrical moments in this poem, which we hope to convey through our translation. We are reminded that there could be solace in freely shed tears of suffering: "You found respite, and even some mysterious charm / In secret sobs, in shedding tears."[18] Stressing now the central theme of his poem Perrault suggests that human suffering can bring a believer closer to his God, since prayer enables him to engage in a comforting dialogue—a sort of confession. It is the idea of "letting go," of abandoning oneself to suffering, of becoming like a suffering child going to a parent for consolation. The notion has strong emotional and logical validity.

Perrault appears at his best here. The thought and the expression are dense and extremely coherent; the verses are strong and almost majestic, with an often elegiac tone. But that is not to say that the poem is uniformly somber. Here are a few lines expressing the feelings of an unbelieving sensualist, completely deaf to spiritual voices within or without:

> A man all flesh and a slave of his sensual appetites,
> Who, far from resisting their powerful urgings,
> Is always roaming the world in search of places
> Where he can enliven his desires, and fulfill them,
> Will laugh, I admit, and will be repelled
> By the unusual garb in which I am voicing my truths.[19]

Somewhat reminiscent of Pascal's *Pensées*, the whole poem is an

inspired meditation, with a strong directness of tone (the "tu"
form is constantly used). The main subject—penance—is never
far. At times Perrault, in strong Pascalian terms, shows that *di-
vertissements* of this vile world always bring us back upon our
elemental human misery and solitude. The solution to man's ex-
istential misery lies in the believer's acceptance of his painful
destiny. He illustrates the purification through suffering in evocations of the Prodigal Son, Mary-Magdalena, and Saint Peter.
The "Épitre" certainly deserves not only a modern reprinting, but
also translation into English.

The "Épitre" had attracted the attention of the celebrated Bossuet, who was also a *confrère* of Perrault at the Academy. En-
couraged by Bossuet, Perrault embarked on his Christian epic,
the poem of *Saint Paulin* (1686). It is a taxing work of two
thousand seventy-two lines, divided in six *Chants*, preceded by a
long dedication (in prose) to Bossuet. The dedication ("Épitre")
is an interesting series of critical statements in which Perrault
tries to formulate the basis for a kind of moral art which would
rival the tragedies or comedies of his contemporaries.

The tone is sometimes defensive, and also ironic. He reminds
Bossuet, and his reader, that success on the stage is determined
by the taste and will of female spectators. This is why "in the
theater [they] can only accept heroes that resemble their lovers,
and who can only reach their hearts if they voice the same
passionate and tender feelings which they are used to hearing, or
which they wish to hear." Here Perrault was suggesting that
his saintly characters cannot be expected to be as attractive as
those of the plays of Molière, Corneille, or Racine, nor would
he try to make his "saints" attractive. While developing his ideas
on the difference between a Christian epic and a tragedy, our
author speaks about Oedipus. For Perrault the suffering of royal
characters in Greek tragedy is the result of dramatists anxious to
please a public that did not like kings. Therefore the stage must
flatter public prejudices with the result that Greek authors
"slashed the eyes of Oedipus to give a pleasant show to that
nation who abhorred kings."

Perrault seems to have misunderstood the circumstances of
Oedipus's blindness, or he refused to admit—consciously or unconsciously—that Oedipus blinded himself. Did he understand

the subject of his Christian epic? It is the story of Saint Paulin, who offers to become a slave in North Africa in exchange for the freedom of another slave, the son of a widow. The subject seems thin for a production of over two thousand lines. The work reached those dimensions through many passages having little to do with the actual drama. Granted that the description of the African gardens of the Vandal prince and of the dreams of the prince are interesting, it takes patience and resolution to read the work through. Marc Soriano has devoted a few pages of one of his two books on Perrault to an analysis of *Saint Paulin*. According to him, Saint Paulin is a symbol for Perrault. The Christian character, like Perrault, stumbles constantly upon images of himself, as if the lost twin surfaced again from the unconscious depths of his inner soul.[20]

If we find little to praise in this work, we can say even less concerning the one "Ode aux nouveaux convertis" [Ode to the New Converts] which was printed with *Saint Paulin*. We find it difficult to believe that Perrault could have been ignorant of the widespread persecution of Protestants that preceded, and followed, the Revocation of the Edict of Nantes. Most of the new converts to Roman Catholicism were forced converts. The poem is filled with "adorable truths," contrasted to the "insane errors" of Protestantism. The "king of kings," of course, is Louis XIV whose "paternal hands" have brought his new children to the "true altars." Perrault, like his king, did not have any sense of the relativity of religious truths, nor of their varieties, at least in this poem.

A more pleasing poem, "Le Triomphe de Sainte Geneviève" [The Triumph of Saint Genevieve, 1694], is devoted to the patron saint of Paris, a fifth-century nun celebrated for her piety and charity. This work interests us because it describes the processions associated with the cult of Saint Genevieve through the streets of Paris. Here Perrault's poetry becomes more specifically descriptive, and his verses acquire a certain concreteness:

> Here, on many-tiered bleachers stand
> Thousands of restless spectators,
> And in each house every window is alive
> With thousands of eager eyes,

And walls are lined with rich tapestries
Whose colors rival with those
Of the gaily dressed crowds lining
The route of the saintly procession.[21]

Probably the best lines of the poem are the introductory ones
in which Perrault pointedly refers to the disastrous winter of
1693–1694, followed by the equally calamitous summer of 1694,
during which there was a crop-killing drought while the nation
was still at war:

Sad and long the implacable war was continuing
To afflict the earth with a deluge of plagues,
And pale Famine had brought in her train
Sorrow, Ennui, Languor and Terror.
Collaborating with the monstrous war
Heaven threatened to make the people's
Misery even worse. The dome of the sky forever
The same had become a shield of bronze,
Still clear and always cruelly serene,
Refusing cruelly to shed even the least
Dew upon the dried-up vales and the burning plains.[22]

Such passages give an impression of quiet strength, as well as
sincere compassion for the French people's miseries. Louis XIV
understood the mood of the country, and after 1694 he consistently sought peace, surrendering eventually much territory conquered by his armies.

Other works of a religious inspiration include translations of
various Latin hymns of ancient as well as modern authors, and a
readable "Portrait de Messire Benigne Bossuet" [Portrait of Bossuet, 1698].[23] But the most interesting work of that genre is the
biblical epic *Adam ou la Création de l'homme, sa chûte et sa
réparation* [Adam, or the Creation of Man, his Fall and his Re-
demption, 1697]. The poem consists of four chants and is seventeen hundred lines long. The description of Eden is the subject
of the second chant, together with an account of the Fall and the
Deluge, which are revealed to Adam during a dream. In the
next two chants an angel speaks to Adam and Eve, revealing to
them the main facts of the Old Testament, the Incarnation, Re-
demption, the end of the world, and the Last Judgment.

Perrault had worked a long time on this poem. He was ful-filling a wish formulated in the preface to his earlier *Saint Paulin*: why not make poems which would honor "the author of Nature and Grace, Heaven, Earth, Hell, the Angels and the Devils." He was once again wishing for a continuation of the biblical epic. The subject has been well researched in R. A. Sayce's *The French Biblical Epic*, which mentions Perrault on many pages. In fact, the book makes a kind of ironic compliment to our author: after Perrault's *Adam*, there are no more biblical epics in French lit-erature—which is not to say that he killed the genre.

While in general the poem is not always inspiring, it contains, nevertheless, many passages which show vigor and originality of thought. At the end of the seventeenth century it would have been unusual if a man of Perrault's intelligence and talent did not reflect in his writing some of the progress in philosophy and the sciences. His conception of God is that of an abstract being, as shown in this reference to Him before Genesis: "Living, and being alone in his immensity / Finding in himself his great-ness, his peace, and his happiness, / Without wishes, without needs, self-sufficient."[24] Sayce is right in thinking that here "Perrault is more successful than most,"[25] and further suggests that through the rest of the poem "God's immeasurable attributes are conveyed in a noble language, but His presence is not physi-cally felt,"[26] exemplifying the growth of abstraction in Perrault's time.

Most critics of Perrault have noticed that *Adam*'s publication is contemporary with the appearance of the *Contes*. It is in the evocation of animals that the writer of fairy tales does appear; some verses are reminiscent of passages of *Peau d'Ane*, or "Le Chat Botté." The poem is lavish in its description of each species of animal. These two lines refer to a familiar bird: "The clear waters delight them, and the swan swims / And admires his image and his silvery feathers."[27] The following lines might have come from a fable of La Fontaine:

> The shy Rabbits, and the crafty foxes
> Hide in dens which they have dug themselves.
> The better to confuse the deadly chase
> Of the hunters, they ensconce themselves cleverly
> In the labyrinths of their hovels.[28]

Adam poses a few critical problems. In the first place, did Perrault read English? Could he have read Milton's *Paradise Lost?* Sayce quotes side by side certain passages of Milton and Perrault: the French ones look like direct translations from the English. It is possible that Perrault may have read a 1690 Latin translation of *Paradise Lost.*[29]

The weakest stylistic feature of *Adam* is the excessive use of the future tense throughout more than half of the narrative. It was the device of the angel speaking to Adam during his dream and revealing the events to come (up to the reign of Solomon) which necessitated the future tense. However, the poem is not entirely defective. It does have a structure that is fairly simple to apprehend as a general plan. It does give a sense of epic unfolding of history, a sort of prefiguration of Hugo's *Légende des siècles* [Legend of the Centuries].

There are some challenging critical ideas in the preface. Perrault explains that in his poem he does not have an active protagonist in Adam, since he is a passive actor doing what God tells him—except when he eats the apple. But he justifies his way of handling the subject by cleverly paraphrasing Racine's definition of tragedy (in the preface to *Bérénice*): "...it is enough that the subject of a heroic poem be important, that it be narrated with the inventions and ornate language which is expected in poetry, and that there happened to be in the subject a knot [conflict] and a denouement, not unlike that of the dramatic poems [tragedies]."

Perrault is original in his conception. It is characteristic of his sense of freedom, and his strong distaste of excessive pedantism. He asks for complete poetic license: ". . . poetry can deal with any subject, and fiction or fantasy, being the essence of poetry, no one can blame me concerning my choice or execution." Once again Perrault tries to be modern. The last sentence of Sayce's book is a praise of our author: "In his championship of the epic and of the moderns Perrault is perhaps a survival of the past and a prophet of the future."[30] Among past authors Perrault does not rival Milton, though he may faintly reflect him; in the future there would be poets like Hugo, Goethe, Claudel, or Saint-John Perse who would give new accents and new life to the epic.

IV *Perrault the Individualist Poet and Writer*

The label "individualist" is not chosen randomly. It corresponds to a philosophy of art and poetry peculiar not only to Perrault but to many other writers of the century that followed the Age of Louis XIV. They were the moderns, in opposition to the more academic poets like Boileau.[31] "They themselves would have been the first to remind us that true poets, without exception, are like plants, which, while they may contribute ever so unobtrusively to the variety and effectiveness of the particular garden they belong to, nevertheless preserve their own identity intact within it."[32] In another sense Perrault was fiercely individualistic in venturing far from conventional paths in the choice of his subjects; he was, with La Fontaine, the only classical author to write fairy tales (in prose or in verse), fables, or poems on painting, on genius, or on hunting.

His "Génie, Épitre à Monsieur de Fontenelle" [Genius, A Poem-letter to Fontenelle, 1686] is one of the happy surprises in the voluminous poetry of Perrault. The poem is a discussion on the subject of genius in the arts. For Perrault genius is a prerequisite of artistic expression, as charm is necessary to men and women, if they are to look attractive. The use of the simile itself is original. In other words, where there is talent there must also be genius. Perrault sets off the simile by stating that a work of art without genius is "like the face of a beautiful woman": "Où sous un front serein de beaux yeux se font voir / Comme des Rois captifs, sans force et sans pouvoir"[33] ("In which under a serene brow beautiful eyes appear like enslaved kings, powerless and without strength"), It is a vitally expressed conception of genius which Perrault develops in this poem of one hundred and fifty lines. Genius is likened to a kind of inner fire of inspiration:

> Il faut qu'une chaleur dans l'âme répandue
> Pour agir au dehors l'élève et la remue,
> Lui fournisse un discours qui dans chaque auditeur
> Ou de force ou de gré trouve un approbateur.
>
> (1:28)

A certain fire throughout the soul spreading,
Elevates and moves it in order to act out,
Inspiring words which find in each listener,
A person convinced, willy-nilly.

In further lines Perrault alludes to the passions of the heart fired
by the beauty of a poet's language. The poet who feels this passion or fire is also a person more attuned to the outside world:

L'homme sans ce beau feu qui l'éclaire et l'épure,
N'est que l'ombre de l'homme et sa vaine figure.
Il demeure insensible à mille doux appas
Que d'un oeil languissant il voit et ne voit pas.

(1:28)

Man without this beautiful fire which purifies and
        enlightens him,
Is nothing but a shadow of himself and his vain image.
He remains insensitive to a thousand appealing sights
Which his lazy eye sees without seeing.

But the inspired artist is gifted with transcendent sight. If he
walks through a dark forest he sees:

Innumerable Nymphs and Fauns . . .
Dance at night in the silent woods,
Who barely depress the ferns and mosses
Under their light dancing steps,
While ordinary mortals walking
Through these same woods
See nothing but deers, does and elks.

(1:30)

The poem ends with a reference to a mysterious palace of ideas,
reminiscent of a Platonic realm of divine abstractions, where artists—with their minds, their hearts, or their hands (painters,
sculptors)—can repair to a storehouse of the raw materials of inspiration to which possessors of genius, from the remotest times
till now, alone have the key.

Such ideas are part of a general aesthetic theory which corresponds to similar notions expressed in the *Parallèle*. We recall

that for Perrault poetry is not a question of versification or meter, but above all a question of substance, and of the expression of ideas (3:280). Perrault had also stated boldly that poetry can exist in prose as well as in verse, and that the opera was a realm of fantasy, poetry, and the supernatural, like the fairy tale. We fully endorse the view that Perrault's *Génie* is "the first *Art Poétique* [Poetics] of the moderns."[34]

At the same time Perrault wrote his *Parallèle* and his "Génie," he was also working on two comedies, *L'Oublieux* [The Waffles Man] and *Les Fontanges* [The Fontanges/Headdresses], which he did not finish and which were published only in the nineteenth century, in 1868 and 1884, respectively.[35] The value of *L'Oublieux*, a small farce in three acts, is its faithful folkloric character. Perrault introduces the character of that legendary and picturesque waffle-seller who walked the streets of Paris, singing a colorful song, which Perrault preserves for posterity. The plot is very thin: two young men are courting two young ladies, wooing them away from two pedantic and ridiculous suitors (one of them characteristically enamored of Greek and Latin authors, but very boorish). In the last act one of the "good" suitors—in typical Molièrian fashion—arranges a final masquerade in which he dresses like an *oublieux*.[36]

The style of this little play is light and gay, typical of the man who also wrote fairy tales. The other play, *Les Fontanges*, ridicules (very briefly) the fashion of that extravagantly high headdress (named after one of Louis XIV's mistresses, Mlle Fontanges), that was the rage for about ten years from 1690 to 1700. In this one-act play a young playboy of Paris ingeniously convinces his gullible father to buy a collection of law books. In reality, the father buys his son's books for the second time, thus giving his unscrupulous offspring the money to organize a party. We find in this lively entertainment, once again, the "young" Perrault. In one scene there is even an echo of the fairy tales. Lisette, the lady for whom the party is given, complains that her uncle spends too much time with a certain Mr. Variqueau, who is obsessed with the story of *Peau d'Ane*.[37]

Like many works of Perrault this playlet is full of quick notations and suggestions. We cannot help quoting this remark of Marianne, Lisette's friend, about the freedom of young ladies in the choice of their husbands: ". . . but, Lisette, they do not ask our advice on that subject and they [parents] tell us that they know better than we ourselves. . . ."[38]

There is in Perrault a satiric vein which surfaces here and there and inspires some of his best writing. His long poem of *La Chasse* [On Hunting, 1692] is at once poetic and satirical. It is a lively, witty, and entertaining series of octosyllabic lines, thirty pages long. The work was considered worthy of a reprint in 1862. We quote the amusing second stanza:

> What a pleasure when rosy Dawn
> Wakes from her reddish bed
> And extinguishes the fires of Night,
> To slink out of the house
> With our dogs Faithful and Moustache
> Which we have just liberated from their ropes.
> Meanwhile, under the cooling morning breeze
> The wife enjoys a second sleep
> Following her first dreams
> Still thinking that she holds her man in her arms.[39]

The poem extolls the joys of the hunt, the scenes of nature unspoiled by man, the innocent beauty of animals trying to escape hunters, and, alas, some of the mishaps of the hunt. There are some charming verses on the occasion of a hunt to which ladies were invited. Perrault maliciously writes that ladies going to the hunt spend a lot of time dressing and adjusting themselves as attractively as possible: "Women dress elegantly for such feasts, / But it is to chase other beasts."[40]

The second part of the poem draws a negative picture of the "pleasures of hunting." Perrault complains here of the enormous weight of the hunter's rifle, and of the unsuccessful hunting parties in the frigid weather. At other times it is too hot, the sun is burning so fiercely:

> That one feels one's brain boiling,
> If not melting away in sweaty beads,
> Over our brows.
> Our mouths fill with sand,
> We cough, we spit wool.[41]

We shall pass over the last episode of the "gamy meal," Perrault's satirical evocation of another pleasure, or rather after-pleasure of the hunt: the unpleasant dinner of over-aged, over-cooked, and oversmelly venison that the host insists on feeding his guests. The poem ends with a gentle evocation of the pleasures Perrault finds in hunting quotations for his *Parallèle*. He insists that the instinct of hunting is part of human nature; we all hunt for the pleasure of it. The last stanza is addressed to Monsieur de Rosières (probably his father-in-law, or his brother-in-law):

> Poursuivez-donc et de Chasse
> Qui jamais ne vous embarrasse,
> Goutez-bien toutes les douceurs
> Vous le plus sage des Chasseurs.
> Bonsoir, puisse cette folie
> Par endroits vous sembler jolie.[42]

> Do go on then, and enjoy fully
> All the great joys of the hunt
> Which is never unpleasant for you,
> The most wise of all hunters.
> Good night, may this mad trifle
> Seem pretty to you here and there.

This gently satirical piece certainly deserves a modern reprinting and translation into English. We consider it a minor classic deserving its place among other works on fishing and hunting, which the connoisseurs enjoy deservedly, sometimes even more than "loftier" works.

Perrault's satirical bend inspired two other poems, "Le Faux bel air" [On False Airs, 1693][43] and "La Gloire mal entendue" [On False Pride, or Misplaced Pride, 1696].[44] What Perrault called *Bel air* is simply what we would call today snobbishness, but a typically French snobbishness accompanied by social pretense; as he defines it, he is not attacking those who have legitimate reasons to feel proud, but

> . . . this *bel air*, this arrogance so common throughout
> France,

> The quintessence of insensate ostentatious Pride,
> A frivolous vanity which moves one
> To pretend to be everything but what he really is.[45]

With humorous insight Perrault gently unmasks the pretentiousness of such Parisian bourgeois who pride on their sons giving themselves airs, trying to pass for counts or marquesses.

Perrault's incisive pen spares no one: he has something to say to every one up and down the social echelons of French society, whatever their sex. He especially scorns those who are superficial in their appreciation of whatever is shown to them, refusing even simply to look at things—like this character invited to visit Perrault's house, who merely goes in and out:

> Here we are, says he, on the first floor.
> Yes, Sir. And upstairs we have the second floor?
> Yes, Sir. I understand, says he, turning
> Around, and going away without having seen a thing.
> All of this, God damn it, is sign of a great intelligence.
> Such an idiot, in spite of his ignorance,
> Knows full well how impertinent his manners are;
> Yet he shows, by such thoughtlessness,
> That he does not deserve to be listened to,
> Whatever he may say.[46]

With a deadly accurate eye Perrault censures those Frenchmen who snobbishly show off in front of their guests by mistreating their servants, a behavior which has been going on for a long time: "How old and very antiquated this kind of misbehavior / Which consists in always scorning one's own servants, / To believe without proof that they are worth nothing at all, / And that our neighbor has better servants than we do."[47]

Probably the most ironic passage is Perrault's evocation of that noble lady constantly insisting on her social rank, even though she was fairly friendly toward Perrault himself. Nevertheless, her manner and tone of voice constantly made clear to Perrault that she meant "de me faire sans cesse rentrer en mon néant" ("to make me reenter, always, into my own nothingness"). Perrault's reaction to such perpetual snubs is direct and characteristic: "I dared to propose to her that we both go to an attorney at law, / And recognize in all humility and once and for all / That she was indeed a noble lady and I, myself, but a mere bourgeois."[48] Such a poem shows Perrault at his best. This is well-aimed satire, more on the kindly humorous level, than on the savagely incisive witty level which Voltaire will illustrate in his celebrated *Candide.* Perrault's humor may at times show impatience, but underneath there is always a glimmer of tenderness, albeit with some malice. The same Perrault who penned those gently satirical barbs also wrote the often kindly derisive fairy tales.

The last satirical poem Perrault wrote, "La Gloire mal entendue," is contemporary with the writing of the fairy tales; it is dated 1696. The manuscript of the *Contes* was written in 1695, while the published edition appeared in 1697. Underneath the printed title of his poem Perrault wrote *Vers libres* [Free Verses], as if to indicate his freedom from a fixed rhyme scheme and meter, and also his freedom of inspiration.

The stance, or attitude, of Perrault throughout the poem could be phrased in the following way: "Whatever anyone may do to justify how proud and snobbish one feels, I (Perrault, or the allegorical character, Glory), am not amused or impressed, if that action or attitude is not inspired by sincerity and kindness toward one's own fellowman or woman."

With his own free style, Perrault reminds us of La Fontaine in many passages. The following lines depict with precision a kind of country lord who thinks he can tread everywhere in his lands with the arrogance of the master in the *Jardinier et son Seigneur* [The Farmer and his Lord] of La Fontaine:

> A lord in his lordly abode
> Thinks he is immensely impressing me
> When he brandishes his cane against
> A peasant in his cabin,
> Causing him to tremble with fear,
> Or when he tries to seduce that
> Same peasant's wife.[49]

With a masterly sense of antithesis, Perrault continues by stressing how much more noble that lord would appear if with courage he would attack a city at the head of his soldiers, rather than a defenseless woman. How much better he would prove his nobility, if he were to help rather than persecute his charges. We quote below the end of that stanza:

Qu'il prouverait bien mieux sa noblesse et son coeur!
. . . si touché de la misère
De ceux dont il est le Seigneur,
Et les traitant avec douceur,
Il se faisait moins voir leur Maître
Que leur Père.[50]

How much better he would prove his nobility and the kindness of
    his heart!
. . . if moved by the misery
Of those on whom he lords,
[And] treating them kindly,
He would show himself less their master,
And more their father.

Apart from their intrinsic literary merit, these lines are significant in that they very clearly show that Perrault certainly cared for the plight of the French peasants of his day. He was sincere in his feelings. A critic would be thoroughly insensitive to the sense and sound of his words if he misunderstood Perrault in this poem. In this passage and in many others, Perrault, whatever his faults, shows he had sympathy for those less fortunate than himself. In the face of recent criticism asserting that Perrault did not care for the people of France, we believe that the manifestly kind intent of Perrault's language ought to be stressed.[51]

What a reader or critic is always happy to find in works that are predominantly personal or lyrical are those passages where one has the feeling of hearing the very voice of an author. The best of these works effectively break that invisible barrier between author and reader. In the few passages we have quoted so far Perrault did communicate, at least, for the moment. One of the wonders of literature are those works which by definition are abstractly symbolic and removed from everyday reality and yet, through the magic of style, manage to convey the intensely personal voice and charm of an author, as in the case of La Fontaine's *Fables*. Some outstanding fables are those in which, through the clearly allegorical nature of his animals, La Fontaine reveals his gently cynical vision (*The Ant and the Grasshopper*; *The Dog and Wolf*), his frankly satirical vision of man (*The Animals Striken by the Plague*; *The Farmer and his Lord*), or his elegiac and lyrical look at himself (*The Two Doves*).

It appears to us that Perrault's achievement did at times match La Fontaine's. But, when he did not equal La Fontaine, he failed miserably, as in his attempt at the writing of fables. One would think that the writing of fables would result in great wit, humor, and poetry when attempted by the author of such outstanding fairy tales. Yet we are terribly disappointed as we look at Perrault's French translation of the Neo-Latin author Gabriel Faerno's *Centum Fabulae* [One Hundred Fables, 1564].[52] Faerno was one of the many translator-imitators, or rather adaptators, of Aesop and Phaedrus, antedating La Fontaine by one hundred years. Most of the fables Faerno wrote in Latin belong to that same Aesopian tradition in which La Fontaine distinguished himself so brilliantly. For Perrault, La Fontaine was a model he wished to imitate. He saw the possibility of trying his hand in his genre when he translated in verse Faerno's fables.

The translation of Perrault appeared in 1699. The volume was destined to be a text for a secondary school for young men of the nobility, under the direction of the Abbé Dangeau, one of Perrault's *confrères* at the Academy. In his preface Perrault modestly begs not to be compared to La Fontaine, insisting that his fables "resemble a suit tailored in a good cloth, well cut and well sewn, but simple and unadorned; his [La Fontaine's] display something more; and he adds to them a rich and delicate embroidery which immensely enrich his work."[53]

For the sake of giving a sample of Perrault's effort, here is one of his fables, in French and in English:

Jupiter et le Limaçon

Jupiter ayant promis aux bêtes
D'exaucer pleinement leurs premières requêtes,
Le sage et faible limaçon
Demanda que son corps fût joint à sa maison.

Mais, pourquoi se charger de ce poids incommode?
En quatre mots il en dit la raison:
Je pourrai me choisir des voisins à ma mode.
C'est un triste et fâcheux destin
Que d'avoir un méchant voisin.[54]

Most of the fables in Perrault's translation are just as brief and
plain as the one quoted above. It is not possible to recognize the
author of "Puss in Boots" in this text. For an English translation
we give the text of a bilingual edition, published in 1741:

Jupiter and the Snail
Jove on a Time had pledg'd his Word
To Beasts their Wishes to accord.
Fix but my House unto my Back,
Quoth the poor Snail—'tis all I lack.
Why ask a Load?—Why! cries the Snail,
For reasons that will still prevail.
Once sure my Dwelling not to lose,
Such Neighbours as I like I'd choose.

There's nothing which can vex one worse
Than of Ill-Neighbourhood the Curse.[55]

We have used an eighteenth-century translation because it is
close in spirit as well as period to that of Perrault. We do not
feel that in its verboseness the English text is better than the
flavorless brevity of Perrault.

We have just said above that we did not recognize in this fable
the Perrault of the fairy tales. To do so, all one has to do is to
read the preface to the fables. In many instances Perrault is like
the two sisters at the fountain in his fairy tale: one spewed
flowers and diamonds when she spoke, and the other snakes and
toads. When one is tired of Perrault's poetry, one should repair to
his prose. In the preface Perrault informally speaks to his friend
Dangeau, praising him for the joyful atmosphere in which young
men study at his institution:

I saw some students absorbed in the study of Latin grammar, others refreshing their memory with the instructions of the Catechism; a few were reading biblical history, some others were drawing fortifications or mathematical designs: instruction was going on everywhere, and with mutual joy among students and teachers. . . . While I was filled with surprise and admiration, I owe it to you, sir, that I could not help envying your great happiness in what you were doing, and I could not either help myself from wishing I could contribute something somehow to such a laudable and worthy enterprise. The idea came to my mind that if I finished the translation of the fables which I had begun . . . they could contribute to their instruction.[56]

It is in such passages that Perrault as a person and as an educator engagingly reveals himself: curious, eager, always an attentive and affectionate observer of the children and the young. He was fascinated by the process of growth and maturation. He admired and envied his friend Dangeau for his close association with adolescents who studied all the better because they lived in a liberal environment where learning was more of a joy than a chore, with teachers as enthusiastic as their charges. Perrault and Dangeau here appear as precursors and call to mind not only the Rousseau of *Emile*, but also the twentieth-century Maria Montessori.

In these last years of his long life one senses in Perrault a greater lucidity about himself and a growing serenity. Yet we wish for writings in which he would tell us more about the death of his wife, the loss of his son, and other personal events. Whatever we may find will appear in a prismatic and refracted light through the last writing he put on paper in a kind of spiritual journal that he began on June 22, 1694 (as noted by himself), and which he kept on writing (presumably) until his death. The work, entitled "Pensées chrétiennes" [Christian Thoughts] is still a manuscript document at the Bibliothèque Nationale in Paris.[57]

The manuscript contains one hundred and sixty-nine pages written in Perrault's own elegant hand. With the exception of about twenty pages which Paul Bonnefon edited in 1901, the "Pensées Chrétiennes" have never been published in their entirety.[58] Before we account for them in some detail we provide here Perrault's own table of contents, which we transcribe exactly:

We transcribed this table in order to emphasize the range of Perrault's spiritual and intellectual concerns. The bulk of Perrault's thoughts fills the longest chapter, "Christian Thoughts," up to page 59. The most interesting thoughts are those in which Perrault voices what he calls Christian paradoxes, or tries to reconcile Cartesian tenets with religious ideas. We quote below a few paradoxes, in French and in English with their page references: "L'humilité chrétienne demande beaucoup de grandeur d'âme" ("Christian humility requires great pride of soul [or fortitude]"); "Il n'y a au monde rien de plus conforme à la droite raison que la foi" ("There is nothing in the world closer to true reason than faith"); "Rien ne contribue tant au salut que l'amour-propre bien entendu" ("Nothing is more helpful to our salvation than well-meant self-love"); "Il y a un extrême plaisir à faire pénitence" ("There is great [or extreme] joy in doing penance," 2–3).

Such thoughts are well expressed, but they do not "rise" to the level of the Pascalian power of statement. In many other passages, nevertheless, we find accents that have Pascalian force. When Perrault asks himself what could have been the meaning of God saying to Abraham that his descendants would equal the stars in the magnitude of their numbers, he shows that he is fully aware that this was symbolic language. He reminds himself that according to recent astronomical discoveries each star is a sun. He concludes by stating that there must be an infinity of stars and suns, far more than human beings, especially in the milky ways: "the number is not now known and can never be" (4).

If we write that some of the thoughts of Perrault on eternity are as beautifully expressed as those of a Giordano Bruno or a Pascal, we might be accused of overpraising our author. We can only refer our readers to the texts themselves, and wish that one day the whole manuscript would be published. Here are a few samples: ". . . we only apprehend the passage of time as a succession of moments . . . and if we could conceive eternity it would verily appear to us as only one moment in which an infinity of moments would coexist and would not follow each other" (4–5). "Eternity can perhaps be understood through the seemingly trivial comparison of what we see when we put our eye into the slot of that children's toy in which inside a cylinder are painted sheep with a shepherd and his dog eternally running after his flock when we make the toy turn. . . . Eternity is but a moment without commencement and without end" (5–6).

The man who wrote such statements is certainly different from the one who published so many trite poems of public praise. We have in Perrault an original thinker who was trying in the depth of his soul to find a way to express the same cosmic anguish of a Pascal, or the same rational exigency of a Descartes. Here is his own rendition of the famous Cartesian *Cogito* (it seems that each generation of Frenchmen has to rephrase Descartes to its own satisfaction—or dissatisfaction). The principle of Descartes—"I think, therefore I am"—is excellent. But his further conclusion, namely, "I think there is a God and I can formulate a rather clear idea of him, therefore there is a God" —because anything which is evidently true can be distinctly formulated, Perrault refuses to allow; for we can have very clear and distinct ideas of things that are false as well as of things that are true. Descartes, after having stated his principle, "I think, therefore I am," should have continued, Perrault argues, by saying, "I am, therefore there is a God" (9).

It is impossible within the confines of this volume to give a complete idea of the wealth of Perrault's insights and thoughts in his last manuscript. Suffice it to say that the work has a quiet, meditative atmosphere; Perrault seems to write for some alter ego, freely and without seeming anxious about the sometimes audacious turn of his thinking. He was at once prudent and

courageous in his philosophical thinking. We would describe the
state of his mind shortly before his final illness as healthy, virile,
and true to himself, once again, endearingly original.

Among such a wealth of spiritual thoughts, we are reminded
of what the French refer to as *embarras de richesses* ("the in-
convenience of too much wealth"). Turning his inward eye on
the notion of whether God is personal or impersonal, our mor-
alist writes: "When God says that he is angry, that he repents,
or that he is struck with pain, He who is immutable, expresses
Himself in this fashion only to adjust to our weakness of com-
prehension, like a good father who stammers or talks in child-
like fashion when addressing his children, and thus can educate
and reach them the better" (21). Once again, this is the Perrault ever so close to the soul of children, the precursor of
modern psychology. In this work Perrault expresses himself in
the full freedom of a highly independent spirit. Here is the last
Christian thought of Perrault we will transcribe. It is a meditation on the nature of sexuality:

There are theologians who say that the pleasure connected with the
action of the flesh is an effect of original sin; but I am convinced that
they are wrong. Because God himself is the one who has thus or-
ganized man as well as the animals in order that they be driven
[*conduits*] in the pursuit of this pleasure to the propagation of the
species, just as He has made the pleasure of eating thoughtfully connected with the need to eat. Sin can produce nothing good. Sin comes
from following instincts [the senses] rather than our disciplined rational mind [*la raison*]. . . . Saint Augustine says that the pleasure attached to that action of the flesh is linked with it like a servant to his
master [*le valet et le maître*] and the one will always follow the
other. (27)

It would be superfluous to stress once again how "contemporary" the thought of Perrault appears, how different from what we
find in his "official" prose or poetry. There is in such writings a
fondness for paradoxical expression. Such ideas are the thoughts
of a Christian, but a free Christian. This independence of Perrault is manifest in practically everything we read in this manuscript. And with this independence there is always a keen curiosity and a wry sense of humor, as in this comment on univer-

sities: "Certain things are good only in the turmoil [*tourbillon*] of the university, as Mr. So-and-So is attached to the turmoil of Mrs. So-and-So" (84). We confess that we are not sure we understand Perrault's thought here. Did he intend to suggest that the intellectual agitation of a university reminded him of the "pursuits" of lovers following attractive women? The suggestion is certainly there, and it has a Pascalian ring.

V Death and the Academician

In the Bibliothèque Nationale is a volume entitled *Oeuvres posthumes de M. Perrault* [Posthumous Works of Mr. Perrault], which was printed but not allowed to be sold. On the front flyleaf a manuscript note states that "This book was suppressed at the moment of publication." Examination of the volume, and subsequent research by Jean-Luc Gautier and the late Gilbert Rouger, reveal why the volume was "suppressed."[59] It was a very imperfect printing job, and not really posthumous; the legal "permit to print" or colophon, at the end of the book, is dated May 21, 1701; and the final registration, showing when the book was actually printed, reads: April 11, 1703. This last date is suggestive: practically one month before Perrault's death on May 15, 1703. We can safely assume that in these final weeks of his life Perrault was either too debilitated, or too sick, to oversee the corrections necessary for the printing of the book.

The table of contents suggests the possibility that the selection of works to be printed was made by Perrault himself. But there is a stronger possibility that the selection was decided by the printer Coignard. The work is mostly a reprint of Perrault's earlier *Recueil* of 1676. There are, nevertheless, a few significant additions, notably the *Apologie des femmes* and the poem of *La Chasse*. One looks in vain for any of the fairy tales whether in prose or in verse. So, in the collection Perrault may have prepared for posterity, shortly before his death, he did not see fit to include his most important contribution to world literature. Was this oversight Perrault's or the publisher's? We may never know. But it seems that in the case of one work at least, his *Dialogue de l'Amour et de l'Amitié*, Perrault carefully revised his text. What he wanted posterity to read was a *Dialogue*

pruned and cleaned of obscurities, showing a judicious search
for the *mot juste* and the best expression of his thought, no matter how trivial this *précieux* accomplishment may seem.[60] We
are disappointed that he did not include his tales. Fifty years
later (1757), in a sort of memorial volume to Perrault, another
editor still did not include any of the famous prose tales, although *Griselidis* did appear in this volume, entitled *Passe-temps
poétiques* [Poetic Entertainments].[61]

At the end of his life, this man who confided so completely
his spiritual thoughts to a diary did not, however, tell us much
about his children. He had at one time at least three boys; but in
the year of his death only one, Charles Samuel, was still alive.
We know that Pierre, the coauthor of the tales, had died in 1700.
We know that he lived near the present Place de Fourcy. He had
long been reconciled with Boileau and probably led a quiet and
peaceful existence. He must have been in good health, since he
went regularly to the meetings of the Academy, whose records
are available. They show that Perrault attended meetings until
Monday, April 11, 1703. At that meeting Boileau and Fontenelle
were also present.[62] On the night of May 15, 1703, he died; we
assume he must have had some illness, but no record of it has
been found.

The well-informed *Mercure Galant* of May, 1703, published a
death notice of twenty-two pages which concludes in this fashion:
"this article is but a light sketch of what can be said about Mr.
Perrault. His eulogy will be the responsibility of the one who
will replace him at the Academy" (252). On June 8, there was a
mass and ceremony in memory of Perrault at the Academy. His
son attended the service and spoke to Boileau who was also
present. We have the indirect record of that conversation in a
letter of Boileau to his friend Brossette: "his son assured me that
upon dying he had been entrusted by his father to convey to me
many civilities and to further assure me that he was dying my
servant [*mon serviteur*]."[63] Such considerate courtesy upon the
very hour of death is characteristic of Perrault.

As we read his death notice in the *Mercure*, we find that it is
a moving eulogy of the deceased academician. At last we find
pointed references to the fairy tales: "Mr. Perrault wrote quanti-
ties of works which he considered merely as amusements, and yet

they are full of merits. . . . His genius was universal and brilliant . . . he changed into gold anything he touched."[64] We have already shown (in chapter 4) that in this article the editor of the *Mercure* did praise Perrault for the creation of beautiful tales. The article is valuable to us because of a few personal touches in the following passage, the quotation of which will practically finish this volume. We call attention to the clear reference to Perrault's marriage as a happy one:[65]

He left only one son whose character reminds one of all the positive aspects of his father and of his uncles, and who shows in his person the result of an excellent education. This son is the only offspring [*fruit*] left to him of his marriage to Marie Guichon, daughter of Samuel Guichon, lord of Rosières, near Troyes in Champagne. This marriage was very happy because of the outstanding qualities of the husband, and because of the beauty and virtue of the wife. It lasted only about seven years; and Mr. Perrault lost too soon a wife he had good reason to love, and which he regretted all his life. (250–51)

CHAPTER 7

Conclusion

THIS contemporary of Corneille, Racine, Molière, and Pascal—in his own country—and of Locke, Newton, Huygens, and Leibniz—outside of France—has too long been relegated to that fringe area of literature: juvenilia. It will not do to repeat that he was mediocre in everything he wrote, and that the fairies blessed him with inspiration just once, because he listened to the voice of nursery maids. The truth about him as a man and as an author is far more complex. As a man, he was a person of great charm, a good husband, a good father, and a good educator. In his professional life he served his country in that realm of art where the results are still in evidence today. A look at Paris and Versailles suffices to remind us that—for better or for worse—the face of classical seventeenth-century France was decidedly influenced by Perrault. This is not a minor achievement. At his funeral eulogy the Abbé Tallemand went as far as to suggest that upon the death of Colbert, no one but Perrault could have replaced that powerful minister more effectively and more gloriously. He further praised Perrault by stating that his retirement was an undeserved disgrace.[1]

Apart from his fairy tales Perrault was a second-rate poet who may in his own time have passed for first rate. It is difficult in this century to understand why. Yet loud applause at the public readings of his poems at the Academy attests that his poems met with the acclaim of his contemporaries.[2] Perhaps we can understand this if we remind ourselves that seventeenth-century French did not sound the same as modern French. What may sound flat today may have sounded euphonious then, under different rhythms and different pronunciations. Yet this sound

160

of his words which we are unable to bring to life suddenly and fleetingly becomes sonorous to our inner ear in some of his more personal poems. There are authentic accents in his *Apologie des femmes*, in *Peau d'Ane*, in his "Épitre sur la Pénitence," in *La Chasse*, in "Le Génie," and in a few other poems which would favorably impress the modern ear and mind.

Insofar as the prose is concerned—and again excepting the fairy tales—no one could today deny that there is an impressive and perceptive series of works. The *Parallèle*, together with the *Cabinet des Beaux arts*, the *Mémoires de ma vie*, and the *Hommes illustres* are the record of a sensitive—if at times somewhat biased —witness of his century. In more ways than he could ever dream, Perrault was a representative of that transition period aptly defined by Paul Hazard as the "crisis of the European conscience."[3] It appears in his obsession with progress, in his insistence that there be a sense of relativity and freedom in artistic standards and endeavors.

It is the error of posterity that it has not read Perrault enough. Yet the recent reprints (twice) of the *Parallèle* and the qualified and pointed praise of Perrault as a religious poet by R. A. Sayce, show that a nearly forgotten author of a great century deserves our century's attention and simple appreciation in the pleasure of reading him. Moreover, the two works of Robert Finch and Eugène Joliat show that Perrault is an original poet, as we have indicated in this book.

Our own analysis of his unpublished "Pensées chrétiennes" reveals an original thinker, a true spiritual companion of Descartes, Pascal, and Locke, who in the quiet and peace of his study wrote down searching meditations on the nature of God, man, and beast: the thought of a true *moraliste*. Turning inward as all moralists do, Perrault must have confronted the fact that he wrote fairy tales. He was fully aware, as we have shown, of their symbolic message. But he did not glorify himself for having created them. In fact, he died without openly admitting he wrote them (others would claim the stories for him after his death). In this final concluding statement we would like to suggest the reasons for this authorial reticence. It is a mystery that we believe points to the greatness of Perrault as a true world author. We will try to answer by first asking a seemingly unrelated question. Why is it that many authors of works that become world classics die unconscious of the posthumous fame of their works?

Perrault is in good company with the Cervantes of *Don Quixote*, the Defoe of *Robinson Crusoe*, the Prévost of *Manon Lescaut*, and the author of *Alice in Wonderland*, to name but a few from a rather large list. What Perrault has in common with these authors can be expressed in deceptively simple terms that only serve to hide fundamental truths about the riddle of human existence. Cervantes "accidentally" hitting upon the intuition that his hero was not so mad as he seemed is a spiritual brother of Perrault realizing that children's stories were not so nonsensical as they seemed, but rather deeply adult, even threatening. In that threat lies the secret. But what secret, and what threat?

The secret is "open" to all: the great artists express it and the listeners, readers, or spectators partake of it. Our minds are infinite realms of dreams, ever active, ever in ferment. In the myth the message is clearly expressed in terms of recognizable symbols. But in the fairy tale the insights are forever ambiguous: at once childish, and yet adult. It is threatening for the adult to find out that the child can enjoy the violence of "Bluebeard" and of "Tom Thumb," the erotic lyricism of "Sleeping Beauty." In that sudden shock of recognition, the child wandering in the magical garden of the supernatural becomes the giant that is forever the brother of man: his neighbor, his constant companion in the solitude and glory of the eternal unconscious.

For the past three hundred years generations of children and adults have shared not only that aesthetic complicity in the enjoyment of fairy tales as works of art and imagination, but also that delightful tension between belief and disbelief which is characteristic of narratives of the supernatural; and they will continue to commune—meeting in that more and more unbelievable realm of kings, queens, and fairies, for at least another three centuries—living examples of Perrault's influence and the reason why this book was written.

Notes and References

Chapter One

1. During the reign of Henri IV, the Edict of Nantes did grant full freedom of conscience to Protestants throughout the whole kingdom. France was then the first nation in Europe whose subjects were not forced to practice the same religion as their ruler. Nevertheless, the relations between Protestants and the king of France steadily worsened during the seventeenth century.

2. See Marc Soriano's *Les Contes de Perrault, Culture savante et traditions populaires* (Paris, 1968) and *Le Dossier Perrault* (Paris, 1972).

3. *Perrault's Popular Tales*, ed. Andrew Lang (Oxford, 1888), p. ix.

4. Charles Perrault, *Mémoires de ma vie*, ed. Paul Bonnefon (Paris, 1909), p. 30.

5. Lang, *Perrault's Popular Tales*, p. viii.

6. See Francis Bar, *Le Genre burlesque en France au XVIIe siècle* (Paris: Dartrey, 1960).

7. These passages from a letter of Racine to Abbé Le Vasseur (September 13, 1660), quoted from *Oeuvres Complètes de Racine*, ed. Pierre Clarac (Paris: Gallimard, 1962), p. 470.

8. See Jacques Barchilon, "Les Frères Perrault à travers la correspondance et les oeuvres de Christian Huygens," *XVIIe Siècle* 56 (1962):19–36.

9. See Marie Jeanne L'Héritier de Villandon, *Oeuvres meslées* (Paris: Guignard, 1695), pp. 3–6.

10. See *Documents du Minutier Central concernant l'histoire littéraire (1650–1700)*, ed. Madeleine Jurgens and Marie-Antoinette Fleury (Paris: Presses Universitaires de France, 1960), pp. 305–11.

11. See "Pensées et Fragments inédits de Charles Perrault," ed. Paul Bonnefon, *La Quinzaine* 42 (1901):523–38.

12. This information as recorded in Auguste Jal's *Dictionnaire critique de biographie et d'histoire* (Paris: Plon, 1872), p. 1321.

Chapter Two

1. James Thurber, *Fables for Our Times* (New York: Harper, 1943), p. 6.

2. For succinct definitions as well as cogent critical remarks on *préciosité* see Odette de Mourgues's introduction to her *Anthology of French Seventeenth Century French Literature* (Oxford: Oxford University Press, 1966).

3. Paul Bonnefon, "Charles Perrault. Essai sur sa vie et ses ouvrages," *Revue d'Histoire Littéraire de la France* 11 (1904):375.

4. As quoted by Gilbert Rouger in his edition of Perrault's *Contes* (Paris, 1971), p. 231.

5. "Le Miroir ou la métamorphose d'Oronte," in Perrault's *Recueil de Divers Ouvrages* (Paris, 1676), p. 62. Further references identified as *Recueil* plus page numbers.

6. "La Chambre de justice de l'amour," in *Recueil*, p. 73.

7. "Elégie," in *Recueil*, p. 180.

8. Ibid., p. 163.

9. Ibid., p. 174.

10. Ibid., p. 189.

11. Ibid., p. 222.

12. *Institut de France, Registres de l'Académie française* (Paris: Firmin-Didot, 1895), I, 37.

13. *Recueil*, p. 243.

14. Ibid., p. 307.

15. Bonnefon, *Revue d'Histoire Littéraire de la France* 12 (1904): 412.

Chapter Three

1. *Le Siècle de Louis le Grand, Poème* (Paris, 1687). Text from *Parallèle* (Paris, 1688–1697; reprint ed., Geneva, 1971), p. 79.

2. Ibid., p. 79.

3. Ibid., p. 80.

4. Ibid.

5. Ibid., p. 84.

6. Perrault, *Mémoires*, p. 137.

7. Further references to the *Parallèle* will be identified by appropriate volume and page numbers, in parentheses, within the text of this chapter.

8. Reprinted with introduction by Louis Marin (Paris: Flammarion, 1970).

9. *Parallèle des Anciens et des Modernes en ce qui regarde les Arts et les Sciences, par M. Perrault de l'Académie française* (Paris, 1688–1697; reprint ed., Munich, 1954).

10. Ibid., p. 11.

11. *L'Apologie des femmes* [by "Monsieur P."] (Paris, 1694), pp. 7–8.

12. *Les Hommes illustres qui ont paru en France pendant ce siècle, avec leurs portraits au naturel, par M. Perrault, de l'Académie française*, 2 vols. (Paris, 1696–1700). References to this work will be identified by appropriate volume number and pages, in parentheses, within our text.

13. *Cabinet des Beaux Arts* (Paris, 1690).

14. Ibid., p. 67.

15. Rouger, *Contes*, p. 22.

Chapter Four

1. See Harry Velten, "The Influence of Charles Perrault's *Contes de Ma Mère l'Oye* on German Folklore," *Germanic Review* 5 (1930): 4–18.

2. See Mary Elisabeth Storer, *La Mode des contes de fées* (Paris, 1928), for the period 1685–1700. For the period 1700–1790 see Jacques Barchilon, *Le Conte merveilleux français de 1690 à 1790* (Paris, 1975).

3. Pierre de La Porte, *Mémoires* (Paris: Foucault, 1872), p. 411.

4. Ibid., p. 412.

5. Mme. de Sévigné, *Lettres* (Paris: Gallimard, 1955), 2:320.

6. Rouger, *Contes*, p. xxii, n. 5.

7. La Fontaine, *Oeuvres Complètes* (Paris: Gallimard, 1965), "Le Pouvoir des fables," in *Fables*, VII, iv., 128–29.

8. Mme. d'Aulnoy, *Histoire d'Hypolite* (Paris: Sevestre, 1690), pp. 143–81.

9. *Recueil*, p. 239.

10. Nicolas Boileau, "Parodie burlesque de la première Ode de Pindare à la louange de M. P[errault]," in *Oeuvres Complètes* (Paris, 1966), p. 264.

11. Ibid., p. 793.

12. Rouger, *Contes*, p. xxxi.

13. *Oeuvres meslées*, pp. 5–6.

14. Pierre de Villiers, *Entretien sur les contes de fées* (Paris: Collombat, 1699), p. 109.

15. *Nouveaux Lundis* (Paris: Garnier, 1861), 1:296–314.

16. Charles Marty-Laveaux, "Quelle est la véritable part de Charles Perrault dans les contes qui portent son nom?" *Revue d'Histoire Littéraire de la France* 7 (1900):221–38.

17. *Mercure Galant* (March, 1700), p. 105.

18. Quoted from Yvonne Bezard, *Fonctionnaire maritimes et coloniaux sous Louis XIV* (Paris: Albin-Michel, 1932), p. 200.

19. Soriano, *Contes de Perrault*, pp. 340–64.

20. Emile Gigas, ed., *Choix de la Correspondance inédite de Pierre Bayle, 1670–1706* (Copenhagen: Gad, 1890), pp. 276, 294, 304.

21. *Contes de Perrault*, introduction by Marcel Aymé (Paris, 1964), p. 10.

22. Ibid., p. 8.

23. While it has been established that John Newberry, the celebrated first London publisher and bookseller of children's books, did prepare an edition of nursery rhymes with the title *Mother Goose's Melody, or Sonnets for the Cradle*, no copy of that first issue of 1781 has survived. The earliest extant edition is that of 1791, published in London. It has been published in facsimile, with introduction, by Jacques Barchilon and Henry Pettit, *The Authentic Mother Goose Fairy Tales and Nursery Rhymes* (Denver, 1960).

24. A unique copy of the second American edition of Perrault is at the Houghton Library, Harvard University.

25. The best book on the subject is still Charles Deulin's *Les Contes de Ma Mère l'Oye avant Perrault* (Paris, 1878).

26. See Pierre Brochon, *Le Livre de colportage en France depuis le XVIe siècle* (Paris: Gründ, 1954).

27. Rouger, *Contes*, pp. 11–14.

28. Stith Thompson, *The Folktale* (New York, 1946), p. 145.

29. Rouger, *Contes*, p. 12.

30. Ibid.

31. The standard English edition of Basile is that of Norman Moseley Penzer, *The Pentamerone of Giambattista Basile* (London: Dutton, 1932). The English text is not translated directly from the Neapolitan of Basile, but from the Italian translation of Benedetto Croce.

32. Rouger, *Contes*, pp. 79–80.

33. This story is still not published in its entirety. A partial text published by Paul Meyer appeared in *Romania* 13 (1884):264–84. A complete edition, based on the extant manuscripts, is being prepared by Professor Ester Zago, Department of French and Italian, University of Colorado.

34. A unique copy of the oldest surviving edition of *Tom Thumb* is at the Pierpont Morgan Library.

35. This story of Mlle L'Héritier is reprinted in Rouger's edition of Perrault's *Contes*, pp. 235–65.

36. André Jolles, *Formes Simples* (Paris, 1972), p. 192. This is a French translation of the original German, *Einfache Formen* (Tübingen, 1930).

37. *Parallèle*, 3:120.

38. Ibid., p. 284.

39. Raymond Christinger, *Le Voyage dans l'imaginaire* (Geneva: Mont Blanc, 1971), p. 134.

40. Rouger, *Contes*, p. 159.

41. Ibid.

42. Ibid., p. 160.

43. *Uses of Enchantment, The Meaning and Importance of Fairy Tales* (New York, 1976), p. 263.

44. Rouger, *Contes*, p. 126.

45. Jacques Barchilon, ed., *Perrault's Tales of Mother Goose: The Dedication Manuscript of 1695* (New York, 1956), 1:133.

46. Soriano, *Contes de Perrault*, p. 153.

Chapter Five

1. Louis Marin, "*Puss in Boots*: Power of Signs—Signs of Power," *Diacritics* 7 (1977):54.

2. Paul Delarue, *Le Conte populaire français, Catalogue raisonné* . . . (Paris, 1957), p. 30. The second volume (published by Marie-Louise Tenèze after Paul Delarue's death) appeared in 1964.

3. Mademoiselle, niece of Louis XIV, was the daughter of his brother Philippe d'Orléans and of his second wife, Elisabeth Charlotte de Bavière, known as the "princesse Palatine." The brother of Mademoiselle became regent after the death of Louis XIV. Mademoiselle (Elisabeth Charlotte d'Orléans) was nineteen years old and a person of some importance at the court. It was natural that a work of literature should be dedicated to her. In 1698 she married Leopold, duke of Lorraine. She became a widow in 1729. One of her thirteen children married Maria Theresa of Austria, whose daughter, Marie-Antoinette, became Louis XVI's unfortunate wife and queen of France. Mademoiselle died in 1744. There are many allusions to her and her family in the *Mémoires* of Saint Simon, attesting that she was rather vivacious, and greatly beloved at the court of the Sun King.

4. Barchilon, *Tales of Mother Goose*, p. 140.

5. Rouger, p. 125.

6. Ibid., p. 113.

7. Ibid., p. 139.

8. Jacques Barchilon (with E. E. Flinders, Jr., and Jeanne Anne Foreman), *A Concordance to Charles Perrault's Tales*, vol. 1, *Contes de Ma Mère l'Oye*; vol. 2, *The Verse Tales, Griselidis, Peau d'Ane and Les Souhaits Ridicules* (Darby, Penn., 1977–1979).

9. See *A Concordance to the Fables and Tales of Jean de La Fontaine* (Ithaca: Cornell University Press, 1974).

10. Rouger, *Contes*, p. 103.

11. William Lewis Wiley, *The Formal French* (Cambridge: Harvard University Press, 1967).

12. Antoine Arnauld and Pierre Nicole, *La Logique ou l'art de penser* (Paris: Flammarion, 1662; reprint ed. 1978), introduction by Louis Marin, p. 263.

13. Quoted in d'Alté A. Welch, *A Bibliography of American Children's Books Printed Prior to 1821* (Worcester, 1967), p. 59.

14. Paul Bonnefon, "Pensées . . . de Charles Perrault," p. 535.

15. Rouger, *Contes*, p. 184.

16. Barchilon and Pettit, *The Authentic Mother Goose* (Denver, 1960).

17. Ibid., pp. 54–55.

18. Ibid., p. 56.

19. In further pages of this book we will again refer to this aesthetic principle in the fairy tale, which Robert Samber formulated so simply and effectively.

20. *Authentic Mother Goose*, p. 84.

21. Ibid., p. 23.

22. Ibid., p. 25.

23. Ibid., p. 26.

24. Ibid., p. 43.

25. Ibid., p. 51.

26. Rouger, *Contes*, p. 103.

27. *Authentic Mother Goose*, p. 48.

28. *Perrault's Fairy Tales*, with thirty-four full-page illustrations by Gustave Doré (New York, 1969).

29. Marianne Moore, *Puss in Boots, the Sleeping Beauty and Cinderella* (New York: Macmillan, 1963).

30. Geoffrey Brereton, *The Fairy Tales of Charles Perrault* (Edinburgh, 1957).

31. Anne Carter, *Perrault's Fairy Tales* (London, 1967).

32. *Histoire d'un conte, Le Chat botté en France et en Angleterre.* Ph.D. dissertation (Aix: Université de Provence, 1979).

33. Anna B. Rooth, *The Cinderella Cycle* (Lund: Gleerund, 1951).

34. Iona and Peter Opie, *The Classic Fairy Tales* (London, 1974), p. 22.

35. André Jolles, *Formes simples*, pp. 175–79.

36. Rouger, *Contes*, p. 13.

37. Ibid., p. 120.

38. In his article Harry Velten prints side by side the French of Perrault and the text of Grimm for selected stories, showing how the German is seemingly a translation of the French.

39. Bloomington (1932–1936).

40. Thompson, *The Folktale*, pp. 58–59.

41. *Funk and Wagnalls Standard Dictionary of Folklore* (New York, 1950), 2:913.

42. Thompson, *The Folktale*, pp. 459–60.

43. Reprinted partially (less the Oriental tales) under the title *Nouveau Cabinet des Fées*, 18 vols., introduction by Jacques Barchilon (Geneva: Slatkine, 1975).

44. *La Bibliothèque bleue, littérature populaire en France* (Paris: Juillard, 1971).

45. *De la Culture populaire aux XVIIIe siècle* (Paris: Stock, 1964).

46. Paul Hazard, *Books, Children and Men* (Boston, 1947), p. 81.

47. Victor Laruccia, "Little Red Riding Hood's Metacommentary," *Modern Language Notes* 90 (1975):517–34.

48. Rouger, *Contes*, p. 6.

49. *Aspect du mythe* (Paris, 1963), p. 244.

50. Joseph Campbell, "Folkloristic Commentary," in *Grimm's Fairy Tales* (New York: Pantheon Books, 1944), p. 864.

51. Ibid., p. 862.

52. Bettelheim, *Uses of Enchantment*, p. 226.

53. Rouger, *Contes*, p. 102.

54. Bettelheim, *Uses of Enchantment*, p. 302.

55. Rouger, *Contes*, p. 129.

56. Bettelheim, *Uses of Enchantment*, p. 251.

57. Rouger, *Contes*, p. 158.

58. Ibid., p. 163.

59. Bettelheim, *Uses of Enchantment*, p. 10.

60. Ibid., p. 304.

61. *"Beauty and the Beast*, from Myth to Fairy Tale," *Psychoanalytic Review* 46 (1960). See also, *Le Conte merveilleux* (1975), chap. 1.

62. This is the sixty-fifth story in the Brothers Grimm's collection.

63. This chapter has been enriched and inspired by many discussions with Dr. José Barchilon, clinical professor of psychiatry at Cornell University; among Dr. Barchilon's publications, his studies of Twain's *Huckleberry Finn* and Camus's *The Fall* (*Journal of the American Psychoanalytic Association*, 1966, 1971) have been most useful.

Chapter Six

1. Philippe Erlanger, *Louis XIV* (Paris, 1965), p. 398.

2. Will and Ariel Durant, *The Age of Louis XIV* (New York), 1963), p. 691.

3. John B. Wolf, *Louis XIV* (*New York*, 1968), pp. 446–88.

4. *Banquet des dieux* (Paris: Coignard, 1682), p. 5.

5. Storer, *La Mode des contes de fées*, p. 99.

6. *Banquet*, p. 21.

7. Ibid., p. 24.

8. Wolf, *Louis XIV*, p. 448.

9. "A Monsieur le Dauphin sur la prise de Philippsbourg" (Paris: Coignard, 1688), p. 4.

10. The "Ode à l'Académie" was published in 1690. The text we are using and quoting is the one reprinted in the *Mercure Galant* of January, 1691 (pp. 135–45).

11. "Ode au Roi" (Paris: Coignard, 1693), p. 14.

12. We are using the text printed in the *Mercure Galant* (May, 1694), pp. 112–30.

13. Other works of official praise of Perrault which we do not discuss are "Ode Latine sur Marly" [Latin Ode on Marly, 1697] and "Ode à Monsieur de Callières sur la négociation de la paix" [Ode to Mr. de Callieres on the negociation of the peace, 1698].

14. "Discours prononcé à l'Académie française le 17 mars 1701, à la réception de M. de Sacy" [Speech at the French Academy, upon accession of Mr. de Sacy, 1701], p. 23.

15. As quoted by Marc Soriano, in his *Contes de Perrault*, p. 339.

16. "Ode au Roi de Suède" (Paris, 1702), p. 3.

17. The "Épitre sur la Pénitence" was reprinted with the poem of *Saint Paulin* (Paris, 1686), p. 89.

18. Ibid.

19. Ibid., p. 90.

20. Soriano, *Le Dossier Perrault*, pp. 201–10.

21. "Le Triomphe de Sainte Geneviève" (Paris: Coignard, 1694), p. 14.

22. Ibid., p. 6.

23. This "Portrait de Messire Bénigne Bossuet" (Paris: Coignard, 1698) contains a few stanzas, somewhat akin to the elevated "official" tone of Malherbe. The poem is really a eulogy of Bossuet, written on the occasion of his portrait (on canvas) being shipped to Prince Cosimo III of Tuscany. Here are the opening lines:

> I want to create a vivid painting
> In which none of your rich talents are left in shadow
> And give in my poetry an image that would last
> Longer than marble or bronze.

24. *Adam ou la Création de l'homme, sa chute et sa réparation: Poème chrétien* (Paris, 1697), p. 2.

25. R. A. Sayce, *The French Biblical Epic in the Seventeenth Century* (Oxford, 1953), p. 193.

26. Ibid.

27. *Adam,* p. 8.

28. Ibid, p. 9.

29. Sayce, p. 145.

30. Ibid., p. 254.

31. Although we often praise Perrault, and oppose him to Boileau, we do not wish, even for a moment, to suggest that we believe the latter an inferior author. We admire Boileau's achievements as a critic and poet. We readily admit that the author of *l'Art Poétique* is a better critic than Perrault. The author of the *Contes,* however, is more perceptive than Boileau in all that he wrote in the realm of the sciences, history, and philosophy, as the volumes of the *Parallèle* abundantly prove.

32. Robert Finch and Eugène Joliat, eds., *French Individualist Poetry, 1686–1760, an Anthology* (Toronto, 1971), p. 6.

33. "Le Génie, Épitre à Monsieur Fontenelle" (Paris: Coignard, 1686). The text we are using is found at the end of vol. 1 of the *Parallèle.* Other references will be similarly acknowledged in parentheses within this chapter.

34. Robert Finch, *The Sixth Sense, Individualism in French Poetry, 1686–1760* (Toronto, 1966), p. 35.

35. Hyppolite Lucas, ed., *L'Oublieux, petite comédie en trois actes de Charles Perrault* (Paris: Académie des Bibliophiles, 1868); Victor Fournel, ed., *Les Fontanges* (Paris: Firmin-Didot, 1884). We are using the 1968 Geneva reprint.

36. *Oublies* were thin waffles or *gaufres,* as they are still made

and sold in the streets of Paris today, especially outside of schools and *lycées*.

37. *Les Fontanges*, p. 271.

38. Ibid., pp. 271–72.

39. Henri Chevreul, ed., *La Chasse, poème par Charles Perrault* (Paris: Aubry, 1862), p. 2. The original edition appeared in 1692.

40. Ibid., p. 9.

41. Ibid., pp. 20–21.

42. Ibid., p. 30.

43. "Le Faux bel air," *Satire* (Paris, 1693) was first published together with another mediocre poem, "Le Roseau du Nouveau Monde, ou La Canne de Sucre," *Fable* [The New World's Reed, or the Sugar Cane], another mythological *précieux* elaboration purporting to show that Venus was born not from the sea, but from sugar cane, hence the softening (sweetening) power of Love.

44. We could find no other complete text of this poem save that of the *Mercure Galant*, September, 1696, pp. 61–71.

45. "Faux bel air," p. 3.

46. Ibid., p. 6.

47. Ibid., p. 7.

48. Ibid., p. 5.

49. "La Gloire mal entendue," p. 62.

50. Ibid., p. 63.

51. See Soriano, *Contes de Perrault*, pp. 289–93.

52. Gabriele Faerno, *Fabulae Centum* . . . (Rome: Luchinus, 1564).

53. Quoted by Paul Bonnefon in his 1906 article in *Revue d'Histoire Littéraire de la France*, p. 654.

54. *Traduction des fables de Faerne*, by Charles Perrault. (Paris: Coignard, 1699), bk. 1, fable 18.

55. *Fables in English and French Verse* . . . (London: Du Bosc, 1741), p. 46.

56. In Paul Bonnefon's 1906 article, p. 653.

57. *Manuscript, Fonds Français*, no. 24, 575.

58. Paul Bonnefon, "Pensées et Fragments inédits de Charles Perrault, "*La Quinzaine*, 42 (1901): 523–38, 1901. Quotations from Perrault's original manuscript are acknowledged with page references, within our text.

59. Jean-Luc Gautier and Gilbert Rouger, "Le dernier recueil d'oeuvres diverses de Charles Perrault imprimé de son vivant," *Revue d'Histoire Littéraire de la France* 76 (1976): 976–78.

60. See M. J. O'Regan, "Charles Perrault and 'précieux prose,'" *Modern Language Review* 58 (1962): 174–86.

61. *Passe-temps poétiques, historiques et critiques* ... (London: Duchesne, 1757). Vol. 1, comprising 460 pages, is entirely devoted to Perrault's works. Vol. 2 reproduces works of other seventeenth-century poets and writers, notably Malherbe.

62. See *Registres de l'Académie*, 1: 421.

63. Boileau, *Oeuvres complètes*, p. 675 (letter of July 3, 1703).

64. *Mercure Galant*, May, 1703, p. 248; references to this article are identified by page numbers within our text.

65. Throughout his two books on Perrault, Marc Soriano often alludes to Perrault as a misogynist who did not love his wife; but he does not quote Perrault's death notice from the *Mercure*.

Chapter Seven

1. See Abbé Tallemant, "Eloge Funèbre de M. Perrault, prononcé dans l' Académie Française le 31 janvier 1704, à la Réception de M. le Coadjuteur de Strasbourg," in *Recueil de l'Académie française* (Paris, 1725), pp. 123–47.

2. See *Mercure Galant*, February 1687, which describes the twenty or more interruptions of the reading of his *Siècle de Louis le Grand* by applause of listeners at the Academy (pp. 246–93).

3. In his *Crise de la Conscience européenne* (Paris: Fayard, 1961), Paul Hazard marvels at the taste for fairy tales (p. 335) at the end of Louis XIV's reign.

Selected Bibliography

PRIMARY SOURCES

1. Works

Recueil de divers ouvrages en prose et en vers. 2d ed. Paris: Coignard, 1676. This second edition is identical to the first, which appeared in 1675, and is more accessible (in national and university libraries). In this collection made by Perrault himself all the works he considered worthy of publication—or republication—up to 1675 are included.

Banquet des dieux pour la naissance du duc de Bourgogne. Paris: Coignard, 1682. This work has not been reprinted.

Saint Paulin, évêque de Nole. Paris: Coignard, 1686. Except for some short selections in *Passetemps poétiques,* this poem has not been reprinted.

Parallèle des Anciens et des Modernes. 4 vols. Paris: Coignard, 1688–1697. The two modern reprints, that of Eidos Verlag (Munich, 1964) and that of Slatkine (Geneva, 1971), are perfectly satisfactory. The 1964 reprint has an important introduction by Hans Robert Jauss, as well as an index and bibliography. Both editions, which are photographic facsimiles, also include the poems of *Le Siècle de Louis Le Grand* (1687) and the "Epistre en vers sur le Génie, à Fontenelle." There is no English translation.

Cabinet des beaux-arts, ou recueil d'estampes gravées. Paris: Edelinck, 1690. This beautiful work deserves a modern reprint.

L'Apologie des femmes. Paris: Coignard, 1694. There is a modern illustrated reprint of the *Apologie* (Paris: Gilbert, 1951). Translation by Roland Gant, *The Vindication of Wives* (London: Rodale Press, 1954).

La Chasse, à M. de Rosières. Paris: Coignard, 1692. The 1892 reprint (Paris: Aubry) is practically unavailable. *La Chasse* should be reprinted and translated.

Adam, ou la création de l'homme. Paris: Coignard, 1697. The first *Chant* had appeared in 1692 (Paris: Coignard), under the title, *La Création du Monde.* The manuscript of *Adam*—with water-

color drawings (perhaps the work of Perrault himself) served
as basis for the engravings of Chauveau and Coypel in the 1697
edition—is now at the Pierpont Morgan Library.

Les Hommes illustres qui ont paru en France pendant ce siècle. 2
vols. Paris: Dezallier, 1696–1700. There was no subsequent reprint of this important work; but it has been translated by J.
Ozell, *Characters historical and panegyrical . . .* (London: Lintot,
1784).

Histoires ou contes du temps passé, avec des moralités. Paris: Barbin,
1697. The *editio princeps* of the famous tales, now very rare
and extremely expensive, surviving in no more than a scant
dozen copies. A facsimile reprint, with introduction by Jacques
Barchilon, has been published (Geneva: Slatkine, 1980).

*Griselidis, Nouvelle, avec le conte de Peau d'Ane et celui des Souhaits
ridicules.* Paris: Coignard, 1694. The first collected edition, with
the important Perrault preface, of the three verse tales. *Griselidis*
first appeared (twice) in 1691, in the *Recueil de plusieurs
pièces . . . présentées à l'Académie française* (Paris: Coignard),
and in a separate opuscule, also published by Coignard. The
original title, subsequently abandoned, was *La Marquise de
Sallusses, ou la Patience de Griselidis. Les Souhaits ridicules* first
appeared in the *Mercure Galant* (November, 1693). *Peau d'Ane's*
first printing appears to be that of another 1694 edition, a volume
containing the three tales, but without the preface.

2. Manuscript and posthumous works

"Contes de Ma Mère l'Oye." 1695. Manuscript in a scribal hand
of the first five fairy tales, illustrated with watercolors reminiscent
of those of the manuscript of *Adam.* It is possible that these
were done by Perrault. This manuscript, the property of the
Pierpont Morgan Library since 1953, was reproduced in collotype
facsimile and edited by Jacques Barchilon, *Tales of Mother Goose,
The Dedication Manuscript of 1695 . . .*, vol. 1, text and introduction; vol. 2, facsimile (New York: Pierpont Morgan Library,
1956).

"Pensées chrétiennes." Manuscript in Perrault's hand, written between
1694 and 1703. In possession of the Bibliothèque Nationale.
Selected pages of this manuscript were published by Paul Bonnefon under the title "Pensées et Fragments inédits de Charles
Perrault," *La Quinzaine* 42 (1901): 552–88.

Mémoires de ma vie. This manuscript, in Perrault's hand, was carefully
published by Paul Bonnefon (Paris: Laurens, 1909). An im-

portant work, which should be translated and reprinted, as it has long been out of print.

3. Editions and translations of the tales (listed chronologically)

Histories or Tales of Past Times. London: Pote, 1729. The first translation by Robert Samber of Perrault's tales in English. Samber translated only the prose tales. This edition has been reprinted, with introduction by Jacques Barchilon and Henry Pettit, *The Authentic Mother Goose* (Denver: Allan Swallow, 1960).

Fairy Tales or Histories of Past Times, with Morals. Haverill: Peter Edes, 1794. The first collected edition of Perrault's tales in the United States (individual tales had previously appeared in print). This edition presents a few minor variants from the original Samber text. D'Alté Welch, in his *Bibliography of American Children's Books,* has described this and other earlier editions of Perrault's stories.

Contes. Illustrations by Gustave Doré. Paris: Hetzel, 1862. This is the famous "Doré edition," with the folio-size format and illustrations which contributed to make Perrault even more popular throughout Europe.

Perrault's Popular Tales. Edited with an introduction by Andrew Lang. Oxford: Oxford University Press, 1888. Still one of the very best introductions in English to Perrault's tales. The French texts of Perrault's prose and verse tales are very carefully reprinted from the original editions.

Old-Time Stories Told by Master Charles Perrault. Translated by A. E. Johnson. New York: Dodd Mead, 1921. A widely circulated American translation.

Les Contes de Perrault. Edited by Pierre Saintyves (pseud. for Emile Nourry). Paris: Emile Nourry, 1923. An influential anthropological interpretation of fairy tales as exemplifying "rites of passage."

Contes de Perrault en vers et en prose. Edited by Émile Henriot. Paris: Chronique des Lettres Françaises, 1928. The best edition of Perrault's tales before that of Gilbert Rouger.

The Fairy Tales of Charles Perrault. Translated and with an introduction by Geoffrey Brereton. Edinburgh: Penguin Books, 1957. One of the best editions in English in this century.

Contes de Perrault. Edited by Marcel Aymé. Paris: Club des Libraires de France, 1964. Succinct and appropriate introduction by one of the great tellers of tales (*Contes du chat perché*) in this century.

Perrault's Fairy Tales. Translated by Anne Carter. London: Cape, 1967. The most complete English translation of Perrault; it includes the three verse tales.

Perrault's Fairy Tales. Translated by A. E. Johnson, illustrated by Gustave Doré. New York: Dover, 1969. This is still the most accessible translation of Perrault. Reproduces the famous (1867) illustrations of Gustave Doré. This translation first appeared in 1921.

Histories or Tales of Past Times. Preface by Michael Patrick Hearn. New York: Garland Publishing, 1977. A reprint of the 1729 edition. The preface is not as well informed as it should be—its author writing that, aside from the fairy tales, Perrault wrote nothing of literary value. But the general appreciation of the fairy tales is accurate and perceptive. Includes a bibliography.

SECONDARY SOURCES

AZIZA, CLAUDE, and CLAUDE, OLIVIERI. *Dictionnaire des symboles et des termes littéraires.* Paris: Nathan, 1978. An ambitious effort. A few references to Perrault.

BARCHILON, JACQUES. "Les Frères Perrault à travers la correspondance et les oeuvres de Christian Huygens." *XVIIe Siècle* 56 (1962):19–36. New data on Perrault's personal life (his marriage, his wife, and her death) from the letters of the Dutch scientist Huygens.

————. "Charles Perrault à travers les documents du minutier central des Archives Nationales. L'Inventaire de ses meubles en 1672." *XVIIe Siècle* 65 (1964):3–15. Further biographical data on Perrault.

————. "L'Ironie et l'humour dans les 'Contes' de Perrault." *Studi Francesi* 32 (1967):258–70. A traditional study of Perrault's wit and humor which applies Freud's notions on wit and the unconscious to Perrault's tales.

————. *Le Conte merveilleux français de 1690 à 1790.* Paris: Champion, 1975. The place and influence of Perrault in the larger historical perspective of the vogue of the fairy tale in France before the French Revolution.

————, FLINDERS, EDGAR E., JR., and FOREMAN, JEANNE ANNE. *A Concordance to Charles Perrault's Tales.* Vol. 1, *Contes de Ma Mère l'Oye*; vol. 2,*The Verse Tales* [*Griselidis, Peau d'Ane,* and *Les Souhaits ridicules*]. Darby, Penn.: Norwood Editions, 1977–1979. A computer-assisted concordance of all the words used by Perrault in the writing of his prose and verse tales.

BENDOR, SAMUEL, BRIAN LESLIE. *L'Evolution du goût de Charles Perrault à travers ses jugements sur le théâtre*. Ph.D. Dissertation, University of Bordeaux, 1967. One of the rare dissertations on Perrault not concerned with the fairy tales.

BETTELHEIM, BRUNO. *Uses of Enchantment: The Meaning and Importance of Fairy Tales*. New York: Knopf, 1976. The best known and most popular work in English on the interpretation of fairy tales in general. Offers some outstanding analyses of some of the *Thousand and One Nights* stories, as well as excellent interpretations of Grimm's tales; less perceptive on Perrault. The bibliography is rich in works written in German. Bettelheim's book has been translated into French under the title *La Psychanalyse des contes de fées* (Paris: Laffont, 1978).

BOILEAU-DESPREAUX, NICOLAS. *Oeuvres Complètes*. Edited by Antoine Adam and Françoise Escal. Paris: Gallimard, Collection Pléiade, 1966. This is the most accurate edition of Boileau's works. Fully indexed for numerous references to Perrault.

BONNEFON, PAUL. "Charles Perrault, essai sur sa vie et ses ouvrages." *Revue d'Histoire Littéraire de la France* 11 (1904):365–420. The first of three outstanding articles on Perrault, which mark the beginning of serious scholarship on the author of *Cendrillon*. All subsequent research is somehow derived from the pioneering work of Bonnefon. The other two articles are: "Charles Perrault littérateur et académicien," and "Les dernières années de Charles Perrault," *Revue d'Histoire Littéraire de la France* 12 (1905): 549–610 and 13 (1906):606–37.

BRÉMOND, CLAUDE. "Les Bons récompensées et les méchants punis: morphologie du conte merveilleux français." In *Sémiotique narrative et textuelle*, edited by Claude Chabrol. Paris: Larousse, 1973. Propp applied to the French fairy tale, including Perrault.

CAMPBELL, JOSEPH. *The Hero with a Thousand Faces*. New York: Meridian, 1956. One of the many books contributed to mythology by the eminent Jungian scholar, whose works are important for a modern understanding of mythology and its relation to fairy tales.

CARADEC, FRANÇOIS. *Histoire de la littérature enfantine en France*. Paris: Albin Michel, 1977. There are many histories of children's literature in France. This is one of the most recent, with chronological listings, and a bibliography of critical writings on the subject.

CHEVALIER, JEAN, and GHEERBRANT, ALAIN. *Dictionnaire des sym-*

boles. Paris: Seghers, 1973. The most widely known dictionary of symbols in France. Numerous references to Perrault's tales.

CIRLOT, J. E. *A Dictionary of Symbols*. Translated from the Spanish by Jack Sage. New York: Philosophical Library, 1962. Symbols explained in philosophical terms.

COURTES, JULES. "Une lecture sémiotique de *Cendrillon*." In *Introduction à la sémiotique narrative et descriptive*. Paris: Hachette, 1976. Pp. 109–38.

DEGRAFF, AMY VANDERLYN. "The Tower and the Well: A study of Form and Meaning in Mme d'Aulnoy's Fairy Tales." Ph.D. dissertation, University of Virginia, 1979. One of a small number of theses on the seventeenth-century French fairy tale. Numerous references to Perrault. Influenced by Bettelheim.

DELAPORTE, P. VICTOR. *Du Merveilleux dans la littérature française sous le règne de Louis XIV*. Paris: Retaux-Bray, 1891. A definitive work, which had a great influence on the scholarship of the French fairy tale.

DELARUE, PAUL and MARIE-LOUISE TENEZE. *Le Conte populaire français, Catalogue raisonné*. Volume One, Paris: Erasme, 1957. Volume Two, Paris: Maisonneuve, 1964. The standard reference work on the French popular tales, follows the international classifications of Aarne-Thompson's *Motif-Index*. Numerous tales reprinted from popular sources (since last century), showing the vitality of Perrault's tales.

DÉMORIS, RENÉ. "Du littéraire au littéral dans *Peau d'Ane* de Perrault." *Revue des Sciences Humaines* 53 (1977):261–79. A semiotic study of this story, within a Freudian perspective, which rightly concentrates on the tale and not on the author.

DEULIN, CHARLES. *Les Contes de Ma Mère l'Oye avant Perrault*. Paris: Dentu, 1878. The best work on Perrault's sources. Reprinted (Geneva: Slatkine Reprints, 1969).

DI SCANNO, TERESA. *Les Contes de fées à l'époque classique (1680–1715)*. Naples: Liguori, 1975. Covers the same territory as the earlier work of Storer (published in 1928), but with the insights of 1975, and numerous references to later literature, including Italian works.

DURANT, WILL and ARIEL. *The Age of Louis XIV*. New York: Simon and Schuster, 1963. Excellent synthesis of the period. Louis XIV placed in his European context.

ELIADE, MIRCEA. *Aspects du Mythe*. Paris: Gallimard, 1963. An important work, among many others, by a philosopher and historian of religion. An appendix of this work deals with the fairy tales as "initiation legends or myths." The fairy tale is seen as a "remnant" of earlier myths.

ERLANGER, PHILIPPE. *Louis XIV*. Paris: Fayard, 1965. A very succinct and readable history of a complex subject.

ESCARPIT, DENISE. *Histoire d'un conte, Le Chat botté en France et en Angleterre*. Thèse pour l'obtention du Doctorat ès Lettres, Université de Provence, Aix-Marseilles, 1979. A monumental achievement in three volumes (extensive bibliography and iconography). Accomplishes for "Le Chat botté" what Marion R. Cox and Anna B. Rooth did for "Cinderella."

FINCH, ROBERT. *The Sixth Sense. Individualism in French Poetry, 1686–1760*. Toronto: University of Toronto Press, 1966. The first critical praise of Perrault the poet.

FINCH, ROBERT and JOLIAT, EUGENE. *French Individualist Poetry, 1686–1760, an Anthology*. Toronto: University of Toronto Press, 1971. Charles Perrault's poetry generously quoted. The text of *Peau d'Ane* (in prose) is not Perrault's, but an anonymous eighteenth century rendition, translation of the original poetry.

FLINDERS, PETER. "Etude Stylistique des Contes de Perrault: Dualité et caractère didactique de l'écriture." Ph.D. dissertation, University of California, Berkeley, 1974. Stylistic study to be read side by side with the *Concordance* to the tales.

FRANZ, MARIE-LOUISE VON. *An Introduction to the Interpretation of Fairy Tales*. Zürich: Spring Publications, 1972. The most general work of the leading Jungian interpreter of fairy tales. Her other works are: *Problems of the Feminine in Fairy Tales* (1972), *Shadow and Evil in Fairy Tales* (1974), *Individuation in Fairy Tales* (1977). Von Franz's works have been translated into French. Her books are not always very well documented or scholarly, they are often impressionistic; but they are always provocative and suggestive. She does not particularly like Perrault, or Hans Christian Andersen.

FREUD, SIGMUND. "The Occurrence in Dreams of Material from Fairy Tales," *Collected Papers*, translated under supervision of Joan Riviere, Volume IV. London: Hogarth, 1938. In this article Freud urges caution in telling frightening fairy tales to young impressionable children. In his other essay, "The Relation of the Poet to Day-Dreaming" (also in vol. IV), Freud wittily alludes to "His Majesty the Ego, the hero of all day-dreams and all novels," and, we might add: "all fairy tales."

GILLOT, HUBERT. *La Querelle des anciens et des modernes*. Paris: Champion, 1914. A standard work on the quarrel of the ancients and the moderns.

HALLAYS, ANDRÉ. *Les Perrault*. Paris: Perrin, 1926. One of the most informative full-length studies on Perrault and his brothers. Illustrations and bibliography.

HAZARD, PAUL. *Books, Children and Men*. Translated from the French by Marguerite Mitchell. Boston: The Horn Book, 1947. This outstanding book, warm with love and filled with the insights of one of the great scholars of this century, is probably better known in the United States than in France, where the original edition appeared in 1932, *Les Livres, les enfants et les hommes* (Paris: Flammarion). The book is a mini-history of children's literature of the Western world.

JOLLES, ANDRÉ. *Formes Simples*. Translated from German into French by Antoine Marie Buguet (no English translation, to our knowledge). Paris: Seuil, 1972. The original German edition appeared in 1930, under the title *Einfache Formen*. Tübingen: Niemeyer. Luminously clear criticism on fairy tales in general, as well as legends, myths, stories and wit. Perceptive presentations of Grimm and Perrault. This important work should exist in an English translation.

KORTUM, HANS. *Charles Perrault und Boileau*. Berlin: Rütten and Loening, 1966. A coherent and comprehensive account of the Perrault-Boileau quarrel.

LARUCCIA, VICTOR. "Little Red Riding Hood's Metacommentary: Paradoxical injunction. Semiotics and Behavior." *Modern Language Notes* 90 (1975):517–34. Perceptive study.

—————. "Progress, Perrault and Fairy Tales: Ideology and Semiotics." Ph.D. dissertation, University of California, San Diego, 1975. One of the more challenging recent dissertations, attempting to interpret Perrault in a Marxist and semiological perspective.

LÜTHI, MAX. *Once Upon a Time*. Translated from the German by Lee Chadeayne and Paul Gottwald. New York: Frederic Ungar, 1970. One of the most lucid and perceptive expositions of the major themes of the European fairy tale by a Swiss critic who admires the sophistication and wit of Perrault.

MARIN, LOUIS. "*Puss in Boots*: Power of Signs—Signs of Power." *Diacritics* 7 (1977):54–63.

—————. "Essai d'analyse structurale d'un conte de Perrault: Les Fées." In *Etudes Sémiologiques*. Paris: Klincksieck, 1971. Every chapter or article of Louis Marin enhances our understanding of Perrault. His analyses, together with the psychoanalytical interpretations of Perrault (by other authors), are the major new approaches in this century.

_____. "A la conquête du pouvoir." In *Le récit est un piège*. Paris: Editions de Minuit, 1978. Pp. 119–43.

MURRAY, TIMOTHY C. "A Marvelous Guide to Anamorphosis: *Cendrillon ou la petite pantoufle de verre*." *Modern Language Notes* 91 (1976):1276–95. A perceptive semiological analysis of this tale.

MARTY-LAVEAUX, CHARLES. "Quelle est la véritable part de Charles Perrault dans contes qui portent son nom?" *Revue d'Histoire Littéraire de la France* 7 (1900):221–38. The first modern study that seriously addressed the problem of authorship of the tales.

OPIE, IONA and PETER. *The Classic Fairy Tales*. London: Oxford University Press, 1974. A standard work by the internationally recognized pair, with copious illustrations, introductions, and a general anthology of fairy tales. Perrault largely represented. Includes a bibliography.

PROPP, VLADIMIR. *Morphology of the Folktale*. Translated from the Russian by Laurence Scott. Austin: University of Texas Press, 1968. This very influential work was originally published in 1928. Propp, a Russian folklorist, attempted to demonstrate, with considerable success insofar as his Russian material was concerned, that the fairy tales, especially the oral tales, had a uniform structure, despite their complexity. He structurally decomposed the tales in various series of simple functions. Has had the most influence in France.

RIGAULT, HYPPOLITE. *Histoire de la querelle des anciens et des modernes*. Paris: Hachette, 1856. One of the best works on the Perrault-Boileau quarrel.

ROUGER, GILBERT, ed. *Contes de Perrault*. Paris: Garnier, 1967–1972. The best and most scholarly edition of Perrault's tales in this century. Important introduction and copious notes on all tales. Presents Perrault's texts integrally and entirely. Bibliography of important editions of the tales as well as critical studies. Essential reference work for laymen as well as for scholars of Perrault. The text of each tale is prefaced by a note on sources or analogues of each story.

SAINTE-BEUVE. "Les Contes de Perrault." In *Causeries du lundi*. Vol. 5. Paris: Garnier, 1852. In this article, the great nineteenth-century critic, who admired Perrault, began the tradition of a Perrault "naive and close to the soul of the people," a kind of French Grimm.

SAYCE, ROY A. *The French Biblical Epic in the Seventeenth Century*. Oxford: Clarendon Press, 1955. The best work on the subject, with numerous references to Perrault.

SORIANO, MARC. *Les Contes de Perrault, Culture savante et traditions populaires*. Paris: Gallimard, 1968. A monumental contribution to Perrault scholarship which must be read by any critic seriously interested in the author of the *Contes*. Soriano's work has not, however, obtained universal approval.

————. *Le Dossier Perrault*. Paris: Hachette, 1972. This second book is a restatement of the thesis advanced in the previous work.

STORER, MARY ELISABETH. *La Mode des contes de fées (1685–1700)*. Paris: Champion, 1928. This work was reprinted (Geneva: Slatkine Reprints, 1972). It is a pioneering study on the subject of the fairy tale as a literary genre. Important chapter on Perrault. Excellent bibliography.

THOMPSON, STITH. *The Folktale*. New York: Holt, 1946. The standard work on the folktale, by the editor (with Antti Aarne) of the monumental *Motif-Index of Folk-Literature*, 6 vols. (Bloomington: Indiana University Press, 1932–1936).

TODOROV, TVETAN. *The Fantastic*. Translated from the French by Richard Howard. Ithaca: Cornell University Press, 1975. Highly suggestive book. A definition of the fantastic based on the notion of the suspension of disbelief and the "uncanny." Various references to Perrault.

VESSELY, THOMAS. "The French Literary Fairy Tale, 1690–1760: A Generic Study." Ph.D. dissertation, University of Indiana, 1979. One of the better doctoral dissertations on the French fairy tale of Perrault and of the after period. Bravely attempts a classification of the classic French fairy tale using the categories of Propp.

WELCH, D'ALTE A. *A Bibliography of American Children's Books Printed Prior to 1821*. Worcester, Mass.: American Antiquarian Society, 1972. Essential reference for early editions of Perrault in the United States.

WOLF, JOHN B. *Louis XIV*. New York: Norton, 1968. One of the rare historical works that can make clear the wars of the Sun King.

ZIPES, JACK. *Breaking the Magic Spell, Radical Theories of Folk and Fairy Tales*. Austin: University of Texas Press, 1979. One of the most suggestive recent works of criticism on the fairy tale as a literary genre. Most references are from German literature, with a few references to Perrault. Last chapter takes to task Bruno Bettelheim for simplistically "waving a moralistic magic wand" in his book on the interpretation of fairy tales.

Index

184